1

Wisdom and Management

Problems & Prospects

Ramaswamy Thanu

Printed by CreateSpace
An Amazon Company

Wisdom and Management

Contents

WISDOM AND MANAGEMENT

1. Types of Managers

Management is the art of getting things done through others. Good management is scarce despite advancement in management concepts and techniques. Managerial performance varies depending on the style they adopt and the impression they create on their subordinates. It is interesting to consider some specimens of mangers and their roles.

The Bullying Manager

This type of managers believe the best way to manage is to shout at their subordinates even for trivial omissions and errors. More than men women are likely targets for these managerial sharks? They think it is their right to bully the helpless victims. The results they achieve are doubtful and they easily create hostility in the organization.

The Clerical Manager

The Clerical Manager drives employees mad. He discharges no other function. He is more concerned with appearances of the employees, how they dress and behave in office and is least bothered about their performance on the job.

The Goal Post Manager

He believes in favoring selected employees particularly women and gives them lavish concessions and benefits at official cost. If favors are denied they resort to harassment by creating obstacles for high performance to employees. For e.g., when an important task is to be executed at a far off port they see to it the employee is denied access to supporting staff or transport.

The Managerial Moron

He is an incompetent manager who is pushed into positions of power by unusual combination of circumstances, often the spillover results of favoritism. Somehow he got promoted to a managerial post. He has no idea of the job to be done or his responsibility except that of drawing salary every month. He manages with the help of his clout to persuade his colleague to run his department, regardless of his colossal incompetence. He tries to be in the good books of his boss.

The Managerial Spy

He likes to spy on employees hoping to trap his colleagues or employees committing minor omissions. Invariably he uses the occasion to increase his popularity.

Tough minded Manager

He assumes that people are lazy and must be goaded to perform. He uses fear and intimidation as a tool of guaranteed response. He forgets that usually his action ends up in temporary compliance only.

The Satin Cloth Manager

. He believes in the inherent goodness of the employees and that people want to do a good job. He may get a response with this approach, but is unlikely to get the best response. In reality contrary to expectations he is more likely to be taken advantage of by the employees.

The Practical Manager

He realizes that he doesn't have to act tough all the time. If employees perform their tasks earnestly and there is no emergency that requires immediate intervention, he takes a back seat and give them free hand do their jobs. By doing this he not only teaches employees to be responsible, but is able to concentrate fully on the most important things that contribute the success of the organization.

The Leader

He is participative and shares decision making with team members. Consensus leaders encourage group discussion about a problem and make a decision based on the consensus. He knows that each idea must have intention behind it, and the intention must be to transform the way people see themselves, to uplift, to enlighten, to encourage, to entertain.

He has the ability to lead others based on personal charm, the ability to inspire trust within the organization. He can't be bought. He allows the individual departments to run autonomously to meet their goals. He expects everyone to use his mind and heart on the job. He builds a team composed of members that shared his vision and is willing to support his quest for excellence. His highly loyal and motivated staff rises to the challenges provided by their leader and continues to strive to be industry's best.

Any progressive organization would benefit by identifying the type of mangers it has in its fold and to design training programs to correct or supplement their tendencies as they affect the performance of the organization. Seldom does an organization get an ideal manager who is fully identified with the goals of the organization.

2. Corruption Management

Over two thousand five hundred years ago the famous Greek philosopher Aristotle said," Law can control only actions and not motives." He also said. "What the world requires is cleansing of hearts and not of garments". These statements are relevant today. We have been witnessing steady decline in standards of public administration. The growing scale of corruption eats away huge resources of the economy. It is said that in construction industry alone 20% of the funds are washed away by the evil of corruption. This holds true in all other areas of economic and business activity though in varying degrees and proportions.

Managers are interested in ensuring that our knowledge becomes available for conserving resources, using them productively for the benefit of society. The managerial tools of planning and control are inadequate to deal with the problem. We try to quantify the parameters whereas the root of the problem lies in intangibles. We can devise controls taking into account this factor.

.Performance appraisal of employees at all levels including managers should include parameters with yardsticks drawn from our traditional values. It is the value system which triggers or controls motives. If the motives are good the results will be good .The seeds of corruption are sown in the minds of men. So we must attack the problem at that level. Performance appraisal should include parameters to cover the following:

Evidence of a desirable value system and its frequency

Evidence of misusing the organization's facilities and assets, its frequency and magnitude

Evidence of dishonest practices and its frequency

Capacity to resist/decline temptations

Family background free of corruption

Life style - excess and extravagance

Evidence of performance violating basic values-frequency

Evidence of getting results by bribing, seducing decision making authorities who dispense favors and contracts

Evidence of leaking out business secrets of the company/ organization

This format can be expanded and revised based on experience. Organization manuals can include policies to deal with cases of corrupt practices. Based on appraisal results training in assimilating a value system with focus on ingredients necessary can be given to employees.

10

Such an attempt to modify and implement the performance appraisal report will be a useful experiment and bring beneficial results to the organization.

3. New Breed of CEOs

Corporate greed has manifested in different corners of the globe. Big companies make galloping progress in growth, sales and profits. They imbibe and propagate the concept of business as a noble profession. They introduce healthy management practices. However, such nobility exists only when ethics becomes an integral part of such a business philosophy. CEOs with high degree of ethics and competence are a great asset to organizations and society. They create wealth and ensure sustainability of the enterprise which they built. They are really Chief Executive Officers.

Business without ethics gains respectability. Really speaking, it is business built on loot. This philosophy of business loot, unfortunately, is gaining ground and popularity. That is why we have booming business followed by catastrophic collapse.

Greed manifests when ethics doesn't support human desires. The result is crash, collapse and calamity. World economy is reeling under this economic malady.

The thrust for such economic calamity starts with recession and is given by CEOs.

When CEOs become Chief Embezzlement Officers the downturn takes place in organizations. Greed and irresponsibility dominate and downfall of organizations and economy with series of chain reactions takes place. We have examples of Enron, Satyam with their contemporaries and counterparts worldwide who brought about collapse of several banks and institutions. Efforts are made to recover reversing the trend towards economic disaster.

For this first recovery of the backbones of CEOs has to be effected. This is not easy unless they learn from mistakes and take care not to repeat them. No amount of money pumped into the system will bring relief and recovery unless their managerial backbone with ethical content is recovered fully.

These CEOs belong to a new breed and they replace execution with embezzlement. Personal aggrandizement becomes the motto and thus society suffers through massive unemployment. Fake documents, diversion of funds for personal objectives, atrocious audit practices, laxity in government control, are all responsible for this phenomenon of galloping greed and irresponsibility where the reins are lost and disaster strikes. If this is not to happen in future, along with scientific progress, management techniques, wisdom should be recognized and elevated to a high pedestal.

Wisdom recognizes ethics and values and is rooted in the sustainability principle which is also applicable to the concept of growth and economy. Greed should be checked. It is here the great eastern philosophy becomes relevant, important and practical.

Wealth should be accumulated only subject to righteousness. This applies to human desires. This simple formula is forgotten in the thick of the smoke caused by greed and craving for corporate growth by any means.

In the interest of posterity now at least, let all business schools and institutions concerned with the economic development take a pledge that they will evolve a kind of knowledge that will be practical and at the same time rooted in ethics and righteousness. They should turn out stuff that will turn into real CEOs who undertake great tasks of execution and not CEOs who are Chief Embezzlement Officers. Then only we can have a stable, happy and sustainable world.

4. Sales Training

..A retail chain organizes a training program for salesmen. During one of the sessions the Trainer explains at length the problems faced and the solutions. He gives examples. One such example related to selling strategy with emphasis on persuasive selling. The Trainer explains an example.

Trainer: Friend. You must always remember that the Customer is King. You exist because of him. So treat him honorably. Imagine a customer walks in and asks for a product. If there is no stock don't say 'No stock' and send him away. You are losing a customer. Instead offer or suggest a substitute, glorify its strengths and advantages over the other one and give it to him. Thus you execute the sale. You retain the customer.

Thus focusing on a company's products the Trainer takes an example.

Trainer: Listen friends. If a customer asks for Colgate tooth paste which is not in stock don't send him away. Say you have another brand which is equally good. That is Bianca. Explain the benefits over the other product which the customer originally asked. When convinced he will buy and you score a victory over him.

A few days later a customer enters the store. He asks for toilet paper

The Salesman says; Sorry. Not available. But we can offer you superfine emery paper. It is very effective and more advantageous for cleaning the surface.

The furious customer frowns and leaves the scene.

5. Primitive Office

Mr. Duck is person who has no caliber worth the name. He works in an office with primitive operational methods. But he has tremendous luck. He survives on this single strength outpacing all his rivals. He gets promotion as Senior Executive. Messages of congratulations pour in. Requests for parties and dinners reach him. But he holds all of them in abeyance.

He is shifted to a new location as his office. An old building with poor flooring where sunlight shivers to enter, a rickety fan spraying more dust than circulating air, table with no cloth to cover and an ordinary chair present before him a shocking picture. All along he had lived with a revolving chair. Now he could not afford to miss it. How can he compromise his status? He could not sit without running the risk of a somersault. His woes do not end there. While he takes his seat the chair withdraws, slides and he nose dives on the hard floor.

He regains his composure and entrusts the task of getting a good chair to his secretary who is now in another office. The latter stealthily removes a revolving chair from a room where the official had gone on transfer. Mr. Duck takes his seat with all enthusiasm but soon finds himself catapulted to the wall. Poor man was not informed of the technique of sitting in the chair. Only if a person sat in a particular angle without leaning too much he could avoid a somersault, .He tries to rescue him by firmly grasping the conduit pipe which slips and strikes down the office boy standing nearby.

Recovering from the fall he absentmindedly orders the chair to be subjected to disciplinary action .On realizing his mistake he sends for the person who ordered procurement of the chair. To get another chair is a time consuming process. So he sends someone for the chair from his previous office allowing for expenses of the escort. He is keen to make himself comfortable in his office so that he can work.

On the first day, on going through the first file, Duck calls his secretary and gives a dictation. The narration of the event is given below.

Duck: Let me see this specimen file. Oh my God! Is it rat or bandicoot? What does this file deal with?

Secretary: I am sorry, I didn't tell you earlier. It deals with eradication of rat menace in a village called

Ratland. Your predecessor proposed action suggesting poisoning of rats. But part of the file has been eaten away by rats.

Duck: Eradicate the file first. Otherwise rats will come again and thwart our efforts. Then inquire into the circumstances under which rats were allowed to enter the room. Their presence annoys me. Immediately obtain a rat trap. It should suit my status. Also get a superior variety of bait preferably cheese. Whose responsibility is to eradicate rats?

Secretary: It is the responsibility of the Civic Corporation Sir.

Duck: I am not here for looking after rats. Here after I delegate powers relating to matters on rat control. You follow me. I tell you another thing. I can't tolerate this dust and dirt in our files. Often I get cold. I think before we proceed a brief on the impact of dust on the thermal behavior of nostrils is necessary to convince the health authorities.

Duck: Secretary, take down the dictation.

Secretary: What shall I write?

Duck: Write "with reference to---.

He leaves a long gap and keeps mum.

Secretary: Sir, what next. You have stopped with "to".

Duck: You are a competent hand. You know what to write. So write as usual with your skills.

Secretary: I don't write to the Corporation.

Duck: It is just like writing to any other department. You write the reference no., and the date of the letter. I shall think over the mater. Wait for five minutes.

After five minutes Duck tells his secretary. You know what to write. Take your own time. You fill the gap forming the body of the letter. At the end write 'yours faithfully'. I shall then sign.

Secretary does ghost writing on behalf of Duck.

Dear Commissioner:

I am proud to be a resident of the area under your jurisdiction. You have been doing yeoman service to the residents of the locality. Your rat eradication program has been very effective as far as residential areas are concerned. But recently I have observed rats inside government offices. At times I wonder whether we have nationalized rats. Otherwise how could we get so many of them in government offices?

It will be nice if you can organize a special wing to root out rat menace in government offices also.

I wish to make a special request. Till such time you organize a department for this purpose please sends one of your experts to visit my cabin personally and lay a trap. I wish to add that the trap should be modern in design and out of view of visitors. The bait should be costly. For this I recommend a shop from where my wife bought superior cheese. To tell you frankly my wife didn't buy it. The shop owner gave it as a gift on the occasion of inauguration which incidentally was done by me.

I am sure you will take appropriate action and take care of the rats.

Thanking you,

Yours faithfully

Duck

Duck goes through another file. A prominent association of senior citizens invites him for delivering an address in their club. His secretary gets a phone call. Duck is informed that the President of the Association is waiting to see him.

Secretary: Mr. Goon wants to meet you.

Duck: Find out want he wants.

Secretary: He wants to talk to you direct.

Duck: What for?

Secretary: The Association is organizing a festival for which they want you to be a patron

.Duck: I know these fellows will think of me only when they want something. Allow him in.

Goon: Sir, We propose to celebrate a festival for the promotion of mental health. I request you to preside over the first meeting.

Duck: What about my transport?

Goons: We will arrange it, Sir.

The car came on the date fixed for the meeting and brought him to the scene of the meeting. He reached the dais. His Secretary had prepared a nice speech for him. He placed it below the table cloth. When his predecessor spoke Duck was sacred. It was exactly like his speech. He searched for the paper kept on the table .He discovered that the other man, by mistake or willfully had stolen his speech. Still he did not lose courage. He spoke.

Duck: I have great pleasure to preside over this meeting. Whatever I wanted to say has been said by my predecessor. However, I wish to point out that mental health is important. This requires relaxation. The mind should be free of all worries and blank. One technique of relaxation is freewheeling. It is wild goose chase. I suggest every year you observe a Wild Goose Chase Week, preferably in peak summer to achieve relaxation.

Before he could wind up his address there was pandemonium in the hall. A massive agitation took place in the city and a surging crowd was seen near the hall. Duck was escorted and driven off to the airport. Clashes between agitators and members of rival groups took place. The governmental machinery was put to great test. Officials were getting worried about the course of the agitation. Duck wanted to take advantage of the presence of a helicopter. He told his secretary that the agitation should not be allowed to continue and the vast destruction of public property should be prevented. He decided to have a bird's eye view of the situation and the extent of damage caused. He took off in the helicopter.

He complained to the pilot." What is this? The seat is so small and uncomfortable. Is this intended for transporting pigs or dumping food supplies during relief operations?

Pilot: Yes Sir. We use it for such purposes. When pigs are not available we transport men.

Duck: Do you men to say we are all pigs.

Pilot: No Sir. I am a pilot. Even if we take pigs I remain a pilot.

Duck: You are impertinent. I will report the matter to your boss on landing.

Pilot: Sir, if you threaten me you will not land. I will bail out leaving you to the mercy of the winds.

Duck: Doesn't matter. Wind is more reliable than a pilot.

Pilot: Sir, I wish to remind you of the purpose of your mission. It is to have an aerial view of the disturbances.

Duck: Do you think we can see more from above than from land. I wanted to relax. I wanted to escape the agony of being caught up in the massive agitation.

Pilot: But you cannot remain in air for long.

Duck: I know. But the agitation will die by the time I land. Duck lands safely. To his astonishment he finds the agitators had dispersed. Duck felt considerably relieved. However he gave a description of the aerial view of the disturbances to the minister, to justify his ride by a helicopter.

6. Time Management

It is surprising to note that many persons do not realize the importance of time which is actually a critical resource. Though it cannot be stored as in the case of other resources, it is unique in that time lost is never recovered. Intelligent beings make use of time productively without allowing any minute to go waste .Unintelligent ones treat time with scant respect as if they have infinite time and they carry on their activities without having the need to meet deadlines. A few examples of time wasters will high light this point.

There are people who solve workload problems with increased manpower without simplifying procedures. The tendency to find solution by increased inputs prevails. If thousands of cases are pending before courts the answer is not found through simplifying the procedures for disposal of cases. Instead more judges are appointed. With obsolete methods of disposal the additional number again proves to be inadequate. The criminal management of time mildly described as mismanagement, in reality takes place causing time loss caused to all the concerned agencies in litigation. The judge asks the police, the defendant, the advocate and the accused to come in the morning at opening hours of business. These unfortunate people wait at the court often without proper seating accommodation or standing place. They remain for hours and till evening no call comes. Finally towards the closing hours of the evening when the victims concerned go for answering calls of nature, the call from the court room comes. They learn that the case is postponed to a later date. The expenses incurred by all the parties are high and become wasteful. The advocates on both sides fleece the clients by charging for the day's sitting.

Take another case where the politicians view the question of employment generation. They sideline productivity of time and the need to achieve increased output per period of time. Instead they focus on job creation. The available work can be done by one person who is closest to the scene of work. For e.g. there is a truck load of construction materials waiting to be unloaded. The task could be done in twenty minutes with two workers directly working under the employer. But they are not allowed to do this. Instead several persons parading as workers are sent by the trade union to unload the material at a rate twenty times that of the fair rate demanded by those who are ready to execute the job.

The twenty persons dumped finish the task but at exorbitant cost. If one tries settlement for a fair deal there is conflict and threat of damage to the vehicle carrying goods .By force of circumstances the consignee gives up and agrees to the arrangement under which the outside workers unload and benefit.

Inefficiency, a function of low productivity and idleness is built into the system. Those who subscribe to the philosophy of mismanagement of time perpetuate inefficient methods on the ground that more employment will be generated. Should we encourage such tendencies in labor management practices? Should any government protect the interest of labor for lowering productivity and inflating costs? It is a sad day if the evil spreads.

7. Executive Obsolescence

Business executives take decisions on problems of production, finance, marketing and organization. They are entrusted with the task of detecting deviations from desirable levels of performance, locate causes and take corrective action.

These responsibilities require basic abilities, which have to be developed and sharpened according to the changing environment. The skills of an executive need constant change. Otherwise he lags behind and results in executive obsolescence. Knowledge of technology and processes, maintenance of plant and equipment, business environment and sophisticated managerial techniques and tools of analysis are essential.

Faced with inability to match needs and resources, the executive needs a creative approach to evolve the right means to solve a problem. Installing more system in the organization permits transfer of functions to lower categories of personnel. A situation caused by several factors calls for different skills to detect and isolate the causes and to assign priority. More specialists are engaged to look after specialized fields of production; marketing and finance .The executive cannot and need not know the work of the specialists in great detail. But he needs to grasp the methods and principles involved in the areas of his work. This will help to understand and appreciate better the needs and nature of problems. While recommending a line of action on a problem involving technical considerations, he needs such skills to ensure consistency and successful results in implementation.

Some other factors are also responsible for rendering executives technically and professionally obsolete. These are defective methods of selection, poor programs of training, poor exposure to functions and work at different stages of career and the lack of attempts at executive development. The advent of computers, information technology, the invasion of psychology and mathematics into the field of business management pose new challenges for the executive. Further the moves of competitors make it necessary for the executive to be alert and abreast of the latest techniques and developments in his field of operation.

Modern technology and economic considerations have created large plants with huge labor force, requiring negotiating skills of a high order. The demands on the executives are changing and superior skills are needed to arrest the tendency towards obsolescence. The techniques relate more and more to quantification of data and reducing the degree of uncertainty in a decision. But the environment is made complex by government policies, actions of government agencies, stiff competition, changing attitudes of consumers and suppliers, and advances in science and technology.

The program of the executive in escaping from obsolescence should consist of review of needs of the job, and identifying deficiencies in his skills to meet the needs. He must familiarize himself with techniques which have practical relevance to his field, and follow the developments in the business environment as it affects his organization.

The executive has to scan the political, social and economic environment for identifying threats to the business. This has to be a regular exercise. He should note regularly the inadequacies experienced in handling situations, classify them, determine the training needs and evolve techniques for improving his decision making skills. Inducting more and more system in the organization releases more time for creative thinking. This means finding new and meaningful relationships between facts. Challenges demand deploying talents for overcoming them. The feedback about one's performance has to be used for self-development i.e. for rectifying deficiencies in skills.

As responsibilities and area of operations become wider, the executive should engage more specialists allocating tasks to them. He should concentrate on areas affecting the organization and their implications on attainment of its objectives. For effective coordination of work of specialists he should have a broad understanding of their jobs. To assess and size up situations and to communicate decisions, faster methods of data processing are necessary. For dealing with people particularly workmen, negotiating skill, tact, and ability to grasp the other man's point of view are essential. This means acquiring the ability to read fast and grasp quickly since the time available for him is limited and he is always under pressure .He also needs to cultivate the ability to pick out the relevant facts and discard the irrelevant ones. He needs to develop skills in processing information, which includes various stages of collection, analysis, tabulation and storage of data.

These are matters where action is required both by the individual executive and by the top management. The executive has to put in his own efforts at self-development and be up-to-date in his field of work. At the same time the top management has to define the organization's goals and policies with a view to promoting executive development on efficient lines. It is possible to achieve these objectives by including executive development as one of the core objectives of the organization. At regular intervals the organization should review and modify its work practices and procedures. These should be checked to satisfy whether they are conducive to executive development. The orientation and training programs within the company or by outside agencies should be so organized that they overcome these deficiencies.

A nation's richest and scarce resource is the talented executive. It is he who turns resources and opportunities into wealth. How best he does it depends on his capacity to do that better and quicker. Executive development with a great element of dynamism is the only way to develop this capacity and to avoid executive obsolescence.

8. Executive Meetings

Business executives often have to decide on company matters through meetings. These are considered important means to arrive at decisions, which otherwise involve considerable paperwork and thus time, cost and effort. Participants at meetings comprise of generalists and specialists discussing specific issues to arrive at decisions for further action. One executive may not be thorough with various points relevant to an issue and his experience alone may not be sufficient to provide a solution. So the pooling of ideas and experiences of various individuals is considered necessary and useful. Meetings make this possible.

The process of reaching a decision in a meeting involves a series of stages. The meeting starts with the points of issue requiring a decision. These are stated in the agenda. Those not familiar with the background seek more details on various aspects of the issue. They are enlightened on these areas by others familiar with the background because of their specialized knowledge of the field relating to the issue.

Soon the issues are sized up and work on reaching a solution starts. The views of others are obtained and discussed. Proposals for solution are sought, furnished and considered. Their merits and demerits are discussed and consensus is reached in some areas. Some members may disagree with the proposals. Some others may offer comments. In such cases attempt is made to reconcile the differences by further discussions and exchange of information. The area of agreement is widened and finally decisions are reached. The implications of the decisions and their impact on the organization are assessed. Most meetings leave the subject at this stage.

Further action like assessing the problems in implementation, removal of difficulties etc., are left to be worked out by the executive in charge of the department or function to which the matter relates. The agencies implementing the decision are identified and the task of implementation is assigned to them. The minutes containing the proceedings and decisions are prepared and circulated for approval or information. In the next meeting the Chairman ensures that action as suggested in the meeting is taken. The reasons for delay in implementation are ascertained and remedial measures taken.

In reality most of the meetings do not go through these processes in an orderly manner. Often too many officials attend making the meeting unwieldy. Some members do not prepare well for the discussions. They are familiar neither with the agenda nor with the needs of the organization. The agenda if at all followed becomes monotonous. Often discussions are not according to priority and they begin to drift particularly when the Chairman is not able to guide them towards a clear objective. Instances are not rare where situations reflecting minor law and order problems arise.

Side discussions deflect the main course of events. Some members speak in a faint voice not audible to others. Sometimes a member, because of his position in the organization, resorts to filibustering not giving others a chance to speak or consistently and irritatingly seeks clarification. The link between the agenda and the contribution is lost. A few members consider the meeting as a learning process. They ask for details about subjects in their charge. When they realize that even this is not possible their sole contribution consists of asking for, light tea with sugar cubes, cashew nuts and salt biscuits. They never forget to offer detailed comments on their quality, color and taste. The result is that nobody knows what the meeting has achieved, the decisions reached, and what course of action should be taken and by whom. Invariably the minutes tend to be gaseous.

Several causes have contributed to meetings producing inconclusive discussions .These are large size, vague agenda, problem hopping and lack of order in the conduct of meetings. A high percentage of persons with the same back ground and experience in one field get entrenched so that their views are brought to focus. The desire to meet status needs also inflates membership. The agenda, often vague, are not intimated to the members sufficiently in advance. Specific objectives of the meeting and the needs of the organization are not borne in mind while preparing agenda.

There is no fear of the Chairman's intervention if the discussion goes at a tangent. When the member is sufficiently senior in rank compared to many others in the group, there is no fear of others questioning his statements. Without a clear agenda the tendency to drift arises. This is more so if the Chairman is weak and members not alert. For these reasons some members come unprepared.

The absence of link between the agenda and a member's contribution results in problem hopping. This makes the discussion inconclusive. A man of relatively high position dominates the discussion if the group is an admixture of senior and junior fellows, the former outnumbering the latter. Under such circumstances the man of loud voice is able to carry the discussion along with him drowning the voice of many others.

Deficiencies are often due to ignoring the sequence in the process of arriving at a decision. The points on which decision is sought are not specified. Information on certain areas is not sought or given; similarly views on these points from other members are not sought or given by them. The same happens to proposals.

There is no conscious process of reaching agreement by thrashing out differences by convincing others about the merits of one's suggestions. The decision is not crystallized and not clearly stated. It becomes almost impossible to assess the implications of the decision or the agency really concerned for implementing it. This necessitates further meeting for deciding on the same points and action is delayed. Subsequent meetings do not first discuss about these points. The decisions reached in the earlier meeting are not followed to a definite conclusion. Instead fresh proposals are taken up for consideration. The result is that points, settled earlier, are reopened unnecessarily and the inconclusive ones ignored.

These deficiencies need correction. A meeting should fulfill the objectives of the organization as well as that of the group, which should be clear about the results to be achieved. The Chairman should see that all members are given enough chance to make contributions. On any important issue the opinion of all members should be sought if the evidence of data already made available is inadequate. . The group should have clearly defined agenda which should be circulated in advance.

Decisions for action have to be arrived in a systematic way. The Chairman should enforce orderly conduct on the part of members throughout the course of the meeting. The purpose of meeting may be to have policy or procedures or work out details of directives given by other groups. It should define the agenda and ensure that the right types of personnel who can contribute to the realization of the objectives alone are placed in the committee. To promote free flow of discussions the composition of the group should consist only of officials of more or less the same rank, except the Chairman.

Exceptions to provide for specialized skills and experience are admissible. Agenda should be framed after careful thought and strictly adhered by the Chairman.

Executive take major decisions through meetings. The value and significance of these decisions will considerably depend on how they are reached and the seriousness with which they are considered. The process of decision making through committees involves several inter related and meaningful stages. The more the group adheres to the stages and brings each stage into focus by eliciting contributions from the participants, the better the results from executive meetings.

The Convener of the Meeting has to decide whether a meeting is necessary at all. This will have to be done with the approval of the Chairman. Time, effort and cost can be avoided if a decision is taken to get the same results by avoiding a meeting. For e.g. faster communication methods facilitate information and views. If the decision is not urgent this method can be advantageous. Using modern technology tale - conferencing can be introduced so that the officials need not stir out of their seats for discussions. All benefits of the meetings can be achieved without any disadvantage. Of course some members will have disadvantage through loss of opportunity for making cash out of travelling halting and food expenses.

To enhance the effectiveness of meetings certain guidelines are useful. The purpose of the meeting has to be clearly understood by the organizers of the meeting and the members. The agenda has to be carefully prepared and priority assigned for discussions. Members who are specialists and knowledgeable have participate as special invitees. Less important and last minute items for discussion will come under 'any other item'.

Some members are unhappy if a meeting is cancelled. They would have planned to attend some family function or friendly meet as roving ambassadors at the company's cost. Cancellation upsets their plans and they become unhappy. It is also important to decide who is to be invited and who is not. A person representing an organization or department should be knowledgeable and useful to the meeting. Views of specialists, if invited, have to be respected. Otherwise it will amount to what Parkinson envisaged. Matters involving technology and huge outlays will be passed in a few minutes without adequate discussion. The contribution will be confined to matters like refreshments, salt biscuits, cashew nuts, light tea, more sugar and the like. This does not require presence of members from distant places meeting their travel, food and hotel expenses.

The importance of preparing the agenda and its brevity is sometimes missed. In general bulky agenda and notes are not welcomed and people don't even carry them. Sometimes they throw them on the wayside while returning creating a sensational case for others to report, revel and enjoy. We will have a funny episode at the end of this article.

The membership in the committees should be limited and if it becomes an omnibus crowd it becomes unwieldy and inconclusive. Members may express opinions just for the sake of saying something and not because they are relevant to the agenda. There should be time sense on the part of all members. Otherwise discussions can turn to be unproductive and prolonged, missing important ones for mere trash. The Chairman has to put his foot down when something irrelevant happens. Agenda should be circulated in advance so that members are given time for studying proposals and offering sensible comments. Brief explanatory notes are required sometimes to make members familiar with the subject and the proposals. A bulky agenda or proposal is rarely read and studied well by most members.

Here are a few funny episodes relating to meetings, which show how serious the members are with them.

One member suddenly walks into the meeting, which started an hour ago. He opens his papers and looks here and there and at others. He is unable to relate the discussions to his agenda papers. On enquiry he finds his meeting is slated for the next day at the same venue. He has come to the same meeting venue a day ahead where another meeting was on. He blinks and stealthily skulks.

Sometimes meetings face infiltrators who just walk in just because someone has casually invited them. They look helpless and are unable to make any contribution. After some time they retreat, of course, after consuming nuts and biscuits.

In another case one member read wrongly the words in a proposal, which was under discussion.

The applicant had stated," I request that funds of this order may be sanctioned"

A member interprets this as the impudence of the applicant and says, "How can the applicant order us". Some others also in the committee support the same view. The Chairman sits like a stone. They decide to turn down the proposal on the ground it is impudent and of bad taste.

More time on trivial matters is spent. Detailed discussions are held on items to be served and light refreshments served at the meeting and what additions should be made in the next meeting.

A frantic call comes from a place thirty kms away stating that a bundle of papers marked "important" are located in a wayside field. On receiving the call the agency contacts the concerned chief of administration. Message is given to keep the papers safe. Soon a special messenger is sent by car to collect it and bring it to the department concerned. On verification it is seen that some member who attended a meeting at the headquarters, on his way back, threw away the agenda papers (300 pages) into a field to reduce his deadweight. This is the respect with which some treat the conference papers and the contents. See how much waste occurred in respect of time, cost and effort. Let us remember these pitfalls and try to get the most out of executive meetings.

9. Achilles Heel in Management

Management consultancy is one of the noblest professions. It draws knowledge from all disciplines. It is deeply rooted in human creativity and free from shackles of procedures and other hassles normally associated with government organizations evolving solutions to problems. Such creative and innovative nature of the profession helps to create wealth in the country. It helps to reduce waste, reduce costs and improve efficiency. These features serve the cause of humanity by conservation of resources, increasing productivity and improving efficiency saving time and cost to the public. The cost reduction measures originating from management consultancy are not a product of locating and exploiting loopholes in governmental regulations or environment but by designing innovative techniques and measures. But the profession is severely handicapped because of the lack of statutory support. Unlike some other professions where statutory compulsion exists for obtaining the services there is nothing by way of any support demanding compulsion in running the organizations efficiently. The result is organizations are left to manage themselves by adopting practices for keeping ahead of competition in professional or unprofessional ways. The profession is not greed driven. The stringent code of ethics is a healthy sign and it acts as a check on the greed of the members of the profession. Fees charged by the members are based on parameters within the code of ethics and not on percentage basis either in relation to the volume handled or results attained. Fairness is ensured by charging fees based on effort and time devoted. The core of the matter is that there is no compulsion to be efficient and no compulsion for management audit. It is unfortunate that this profession, though of comparatively recent origin, is not given due recognition by the government taking into account the area for immense benefits at minimum cost Management function is taken lightly and the feeling goes around in many organizations that square pegs can be fitted into round holes. Many are aware that there is a high density cobweb of incompetence in many organizations where efficiency is compromised on populist grounds. But even within the limitations of populist considerations, considerable improvement can be achieved if a degree of compulsion is enforced by way of statutory management audit. This will bring into light unhealthy, harmful management practices in all areas of management. By proper installation of management controls corruption can be minimized .This is easier with the introduction of information technology which helps to reduce the time for mischievous thinking and exercise of discretion in violation of accepted norms and propriety. Till the authorities become aware of the need and act for such a statutory measure, the profession will have to fend for itself relying on its ethics and on the maxim that the sun does not require any certificate to prove its credentials to shine and radiate light. The absence of compulsory management audit acts as the Achilles heel in the profession of management consultants retarding its growth. Apex professional could take up the noble cause with grit and determination to succeed.

10. Vitalizing Top Management

Early 21st century witnessed corporate scandals, corporate greed, selfishness, incompetence, corruption and increasing criminalization of corporate behavior. Crisis in board rooms in many major companies showed symptoms of corporate collapse. There were cases of abuse of office for personal and political gain and directorial corruption with the result public confidence eroded. Public's growing intolerance of directorial ignorance and incompetence in major companies in Western Countries e.g. France and Italy, called for growing demands for corporate accountability. The vast majority of directors admitted they had no training. Demands for transparency from the public resulted in seeking political intervention in corporate affairs.

Eminent experts suggested several essential measures for improving the competence of the Board of Directors. Some of these are a Learning Board with mission, vision, values and ethics, creation of an emotional and cultural climate and steps for monitoring the external environment. They call for completely different thinking skills, strategic thinking and accountability. The practices in different European countries are examined and methods of board training and development outlined.

Assessment of performance of directors, development agenda and developing crucial skills are highlighted. There is emphasis on the need for transparency, transformation and for developing Directors' competencies.

The recommendations provide for a program of learning and clear and intelligent advice on how to improve the performance of the board. They emphasize the need to curb greed and impart ethics and values in corporate management with the examples of Enron and some major companies in European countries

The Board has to function as an effective, reflecting, debating and decision making group with excellence and commitment. It has to set example of predominant values for the organization as a whole. The suggestions cover setting up Centers of excellence for director development, developing relevant attitude and skills for directing the enterprise with integrity. They call for professionalization of directors, a system for director accreditation and registration, establishment of Learning Boards and for ensuring accountability, transparency, and restoring public confidence in addition to a combined code of corporate governance. These measures serve go a long way to achieve effective corporate governance

11. Time as a Prime Resource

Time is the measurement of interval between two events or experiences. Unlike other factors it is a fixed one. If not rightly used for thought or action it is a waste, never to be recovered. An executive has always to think of action. The relevant experiences before such an action have an effect on the nature of action taken during such an interval.

Similarly the experience during the time under consideration definitely leaves a result depending on the soundness of action taken during that period. So to ensure that subsequent periods bring desirable, tangible and beneficial results, like any other resource, time available should be intelligently utilized.

Time is non-recoverable and hence a critical resource. The other resources are men, materials, machines and money. These resources in different combinations, within a time span, produce results. They are achieved with reference to definite needs, which have been identified. So a business executive has to match the needs and resources in relation to the time available for achieving definite results. If such time is not available he will have to use more of other resources within the available time.

An executive takes decisions triggering actions to achieve pre-determined results. Action leads to consequences, which reflect also the forces of the environment. Speedy decisions bring quicker actions and results. Whether the decision is right or wrong depends on the soundness of the process up to the decision making level. These processes in turn depend on the marshalling of facts relevant to the decision before the time of action.

For a business executive action has to be always in terms of results to be achieved as stated by the management through clear objectives. The time available to him, apart from that for his personal and family needs, should be solely used for the growth of his organization. Such time will also include time needed for self-improvement and proficiency in job. His thoughts can directly be canalized towards his managerial functions. Once the planning stage is over he acts mostly through the team working with him

While discharging his official duties he should always remember these relationships in the organization, the functions directly under his charge and the main objectives of the organization. Within a given time he can achieve results. This depends upon his mental and intellectual equipment and how he acts or makes use of his available time. While this is what one normally expects from an executive, let us consider what actually happens in reality.

There are several instances where executives work in a leisurely manner. There may be too many men, which often causes clash of priorities. In addition constraints of environment and procedures consume most of the available time. Absence of a system necessitates consideration of a matter in a repetitive time consuming way of trial and error. Executives find time hanging on them and the absence of a creative outlook towards life and work causes boredom.

Inadequate communication facilities or lack of supplies consume much time adversely affecting results. A loose organization results in wastage of time on knowing who is doing what, who has authority to do, and who the person to be contacted etc is. Even with all these the absence of a clear goal dissipates the efforts of the staff. There is no sense of urgency; no order of priority and absence of constant review with the result the time element in producing results are forgotten.

These factors mainly arise due to lack of clear objectives. If not all departments will function efficiently considering the time availability and work schedule. There are other contributory factors. These are ignorance of employees about the value of time, incompetence, and absence of essential facilities, indiscipline, and presence of square pegs in round holes and the lack of recognition for good ideas.

Further an executive's time is wasted if he is regularly used for a job, which could be done by another on lower salary. This practice of exploiting an executive's presence to do an absentee's work, irrespective of job content, is a poor method of using his time.

Square pegs in round holes may refuse to be convinced and give excuses for not getting things done. One important point for executives to remember is that some employees exploit the facility of free access to their bosses. Forgetting the value of time for the bosses, they introduce in the conversation questions, seeking details like color, shape and weight of tomatoes in South American countries and how vegetable cutlets are prepared in Antarctica.

This may be a source of adding to their general knowledge. But imagine how much time is axed by such questions particularly when answered. If the boss ventures to tolerate this, the disease will spread and contaminate others. If the proportion of such personnel increases in the organization, the executive with a creative mind will find his creativity choked. Thus wordlessness is an enemy of efficiency. It makes serious inroads into the precious time of those who value their time

Now let us consider the solution to the problem of time squeeze, though it can be only a partial remedy. The prime need of the executive should be to regard time as a resource. In fact it should be given the importance of a critical resource in management since it is more precious than any other resource. Once lost it can never be recovered or substituted. He can effectively manage time over which he has full control provided he knows how to manage its use. For this he should obtain essential facilities particularly for communication. The management should recognize the need for such facilities and offer them voluntarily and ungrudgingly rather than waiting to give them after repeated demands and bargaining.

The objectives of the executive should be:

1. To save time by releasing time from unproductive and less important activities and

2. To get the maximum results per period.

It is useful to examine how these objectives could be achieved. Faster movement, speedy decisions and removing constrains in work help to save time.

The executive should ensure means of faster communication, clear and simpler procedures and minimum inter personal and departmental consultation. He should minimize constrains and introduce system into his official and personal life so that decisions are made as a routine activity, releasing time for more important and complex work. He should have a clear and definite goal and all other sub goals directed towards it.

He should canalize his efforts and those of his subordinates in furthering the main goal and constantly improve his competence to excel in his job. Through self-improvement and developing subordinates he will have more time for creative and productive work.

For realizing most out of each minute he should plan ahead the needs, use of resources and the use of time. Thus at the time of action he can double his output.

The executive should organize his efforts to adhere to the schedule. It is necessary for him to be up-to-date with information relevant to his field of work. This enables him to save time, which otherwise is spent in hunting for the material at the last minute. Above all he should work out the most efficient way of getting a job done. He should identify deviations from standards, analyze them and minimize the time for corrective action. Management should give him authority to command necessary resources.

An executive by his own efforts cannot achieve the best results from the use of his time, although he forms part of the management. The organization has to be molded to achieve such a purpose. The company has to provide executives all facilities essential to achieve the goal of the organization. Only then managers can manage time effectively and productively.

12. The Human Mind

Of all faculties of man, the mind is a remarkable one, a 10 billion dollar gift. It is said that if a machine is to be made to discharge the functions of the mind, it will cost at least $10 billion. Even then it will be a poor substitute for the mind, which travels faster than light. The moment you desire to be in a distant 5 billion light years away your mind takes you there. When we are blessed with such a precious gift, we have to ask ourselves whether we making the best use of it for the benefit of society and us. The answer is 'No'.

The mind is a flow of thoughts occurring at random and sometimes with a purpose. It entertains negative and positive thoughts on different occasions. It has great potential for doing good and bad. Sometimes it is dull and at other times it is very active. It is restless and this aggravates if neglected. There is a case of a monkey to illustrate the seriousness of the restless mind. The monkey by itself is restless. It got intoxicated with liquor. In that condition a scorpion stung it. On the way it was seized by a devil. Now you can imagine its condition as a result of the cumulative impact of all these influences. So is the case with the human mind, which is uncared and nurtured with thoughts of anger and greed. We have sense organs for hearing, seeing, tasting, touching and smelling. Without the mind these organs are only matter. It is the mind behind the organs that makes them functional.

The choice of thoughts is decided by the intellect, which weighs pros and cons, discriminates and decides. The seeds of wars are sown in the minds of men. This shows its destructive nature. The seeds of good deeds also originate in the mind and they form one's character and ultimately destiny. We have seen great scientists and leaders who applied their minds positively upholding noble and lofty ideals, ultimately bringing about great inventions, discoveries and achievements. We are not really attaining the potential of the mind. Except in rare cases, Hardly 0.1 per cent of it is utilized Human beings who have achieved high are those who have tapped the reservoir of energy within. Others fritter away such energy in ephemeral pleasures, entertainments, time wasting occupations, nonsensical conversation and gossip, which benefit none. The mind is a double-edged sword that can be use for killing an enemy or save a person. The great achievements of Nobel laureates reveal the positive and fruitful use of mind whereas those using destructive means reveal negative applications. Great men control the mind, conserve energy to benefit society and get a sense of fulfillment. They develop powers of concentration. Meditation helps to control the mind by focusing on a single idea or object on which thought flows without any break.

Intelligent men believe in living in the present. It is worth realizing that the present alone is within our control. The past is gone. We have no control over it. Today's present becomes tomorrow's past. Today's future becomes tomorrow present. So there is no past or future but only present. We must productively use the present moment before us and live in the present to get the best results from our efforts. We should not have preoccupations. . It does not mean we should not think of the future or learn from the past. We can learn lessons from the past to make improvements in the present, which will have impact on the future. We can plan for the future to devote our time usefully. Future is shaped by what we do in the present.

Desire originates in mind. If allowed to go unchecked it multiplies and creates agitations dissipating energy. If desires are not fulfilled anger arises and mental agitation follows. A satisfied desire leads to craving and soon greed overtakes us. All these depict the unbridled condition of the mind resulting in mental ill health and unhappiness. So we have to keep the mind steady and calm.

There is a beautiful example given in the Hindu scriptures, which makes us understand the role of the mind. The human body is compared to a chariot. The five senses are the horses and the reins represent the mind. The charioteer is the intellect. The occupant is God who is the witness to everything. For excellence in performance the senses have to be controlled. The mind does this under proper control and direction. For effective functioning it has to take orders from the intellect, which directs it without allowing going astray. When this happens harmoniously the chariot goes smoothly along the right royal road and to the destination.

It is important for all and particularly for business executives to keep the mind steady and calm. Executives suffer stress, which is an undesirable experience. Everyone wants relief from stress. It clouds ones thinking, saps energy and health. The result is that a stress-affected person explodes out of bad temper. Some executives howl like wild beasts at subordinates and believe in the practice of animal control. This sets in motion a chain reaction and strained relationships in the organization. Progressive organizations will do well to include meditation as part of management techniques to attain human excellence and organizational harmony. They can control executive behavior molding it for organizational effectiveness. Laughter relaxes the mind and is the best medicine to relief stress. It costs nothing. Just like air, space, water, fire and earth it is free. The mind becomes fresh. Laugher tones up the system. Laughter therapy has come to be accepted as a useful technique for attaining mental health and harmony. Let us realize and fully utilize the great gift God has bestowed on us. Great achievers in any field are those who realized this potential and developed a universal mind. Let us move in that direction and inspire posterity. Thus we build a better world to live and enjoy.

13. Ancient Wisdom

Management is the art of attaining definite objectives often with inadequate resources. Mankind owes so much to Bhagavad-Gita for its teachings many of which have management implications particularly in the area of human resources development. The economy of a nation is the karma (action) of its business leaders. There is nothing higher than the Bhagavad Gita as a source of motivation and excellence for nation building and leadership development. The economic future of any country rests on the young managers of today. Only men of character and vision deeply rooted in management and spiritual strength can make a nation culturally and economically strong. This should be the goal and message of modern management.

Many managers feel rudderless for want of a proper value system. Pressure groups gain ascendancy in organizations and in society. They displace sanity, reason and love and install corruption, incompetence and greed in their place. We have come across several cases in support of this phenomenon. In pursuit of wealth they neglect their own duty to society. Violence and frustration, give rise to constant mental conflict and intellect is clouded. Agitations and strikes plague society and work havoc causing huge erosion of resources. The result is substandard performance in all areas of activity and wastage of resources. This is exactly what management and wisdom seek to avoid.

The rudderless performance is the result of imbalance in the body, mind and intellect system. Expectations grow fast and are not fulfilled. The enormous intangible resource within man is not tapped and its potential not realized. This reservoir of talent and energy is mostly wasted. . In short we are not managing our God given internal resources effectively and for the benefit of society.

What is the remedy? Management. Yes, Management that will rely on ancient Indian wisdom, which is the world's precious and priceless heritage. It emphasizes the need for mind control, positive thinking and a healthy body.

Here comes the role of self-management. Spirituality provides insight into the knowledge of "knowledge". Management is the noblest of noble professions. Both are creative. Both stress on optimum resource utilization. Our objective should be to excel in a chosen field for activity. All of us want happiness, which is a state of mind. It does not mean the joy of possessing material objects. It is attaining peace of mind and remaining in that state without any break. In that state of mind great contributions to society take place. The examples of great leaders reveal their strength derived from the inspiration sprouting from the bottom of the reservoir of wisdom evolved from spiritual strength.

What should we do? The concept of empathy widely discussed in management can be extended to include respect for all. It is respecting the human side of enterprise. It is enlarging the scope of the Y theory of Mc Gregor, an authority on human relations. We must learn to love all creations in the universe. Our environmentalists discovered the need for conservation of natural wealth only recently whereas Indian sages (Rishis) discovered and propagated this concept thousands of years ago. We must stretch our minds to the farthest limit. The mind is a $10 billion gift. Here the concept of developing a universal mind becomes relevant. It is an extension of the management concept of thinking big. It is the highest development of the concept of conceptual skill. Conserving our energy and cultivating positive values will greatly help the cause of management. We must seek and master the true knowledge, the knowledge of all knowledge, and the light of all lights. This is royal wisdom. It is the purifier, which will help to liquidate all evil tendencies in the mind. There will be no source of disturbance and one can attain total freedom from stress, which is a curse of the modern executive. It enables one to discharge all obligatory duties faithfully. One's intellect will be calm and peace sets in. One will not entertain any greed prompted thought.

Take care of the body through yoga, pranayama and control of food. Yoga asana with proper breathing will ensure stamina, efficiency and good health. By living in the present one can manage time better and make it more productive. This concept of time management is deeply imbedded in ancient Indian wisdom. One will be free from preoccupations. One will not regret about the mistakes of the past or have anxieties about the future. One can aim at excellence cherishing age-old time-tested values. Spiritual strength is the greatest asset. A manager benefits considerably by developing and holding on to it. It helps to develop muscles of iron and nerves of steel.

It is worth remembering the old saying "Better a moment of glow than a lifetime of smoke". Thus we achieve a better quality of life and TQM.This should be the message to young managers. Modern management will gain a lot if it brings spirituality in its fold as part of a systems approach to efficient value based management

14. Management Consulting

Being a noble profession, management consultancy welcomes knowledge from all disciplines and areas of knowledge for solution of managerial problems. It has benefited considerably by opening its doors to welcome knowledge from many areas. It has contributed to the enrichment of the management profession by formulating approaches having wide applications.

However, it is sad to note that the most promising source of strength for the profession to benefit organizations and humanity has not been given adequate importance. The purpose of this series of articles is to bring out the quintessence of the knowledge, -vital for value creation, innovation and knowledge management.

Value creation is creating value by applying knowledge available to us in any area of human activity with a management orientation. This is to bring about productive and useful results in organizations benefiting several people. . Innovation is bringing out something new but which can revolutionize our ways of living.

Knowledge management is managing or making use of available knowledge for attaining definite objectives. Management consultancy has the objective of designing and applying concepts, tools and techniques for the improved performance of organizations. This has to be consistent with ethics and resource availability.

Let us consider for a while what is happening to value creation? Here it is worthwhile raising a few questions. Are we creating value always to attain the maximum potential? In terms of monetary and production value we are adding to value. But in terms of consumer satisfaction, happiness and sustainability of resources are we adding value? Are we not producing low priority goods and services on the pretext of economic growth? Is there not tacit consent given to unethical ways of facing competition and making profits in the garb of sophisticated terms?

In reality there is knowledge explosion but not always in the right direction. We all ideally aim that this knowledge should benefit a vast majority of people. Knowledge is not required for knowledge sake. It should be sustainable knowledge. It should be such that its growth has to be only to the extent ethics support it. Otherwise that knowledge becomes harmful or redundant.

In effect a small section of people benefit substantially and the others get marginal benefit. It is this distorted knowledge management that restricts the field of operations of management consultancy confining it to industry and organizations.

We talk about systems approach for solving problems. This envisages a total approach to problem solving using relevant knowledge from all disciplines considering the system and subsystems. But have we seriously tried to use relevant valuable knowledge from spirituality-based sources, which constitute a subsystem of knowledge? These sources originate from ancient scriptures of wisdom, which greatly emphasize human excellence. They focus on the individual. We know human resources are very important. We all appreciate the role of motivation in achieving performance. But do we recognize the power within man to excel in performance and how this could be tapped and realized in terms of potential. This is an omission needing immediate attention and correction.

This vital knowledge is available to us for thousands of years. Great sages of vision, who had only the good of humanity in mind, evolved this. There is very little evidence of the quintessence of our ancient wisdom being used by the management consultancy profession in an organized manner.

It is the spirit within man, which makes living possible and in whose presence alone all human action and achievement are possible. It is the divinity that really illumines the functioning of the body. It imparts strength to men and managers if they realize its presence and are attached to it. The thought that one is the spirit gives strength and this is a vital force, which motivates. It helps to view the body as an instrument of action. It propels one to excel in performance without craving for rewards.

The inspiration one gets from such a faith is tremendous. This created many leaders in India and abroad. They shook the world with their power of thoughts and actions. Such men had a conceptual approach not confined to any organization but to the whole country and even beyond. It is this approach that gave them a vision and dynamism to achieve human excellence. They were real leaders worthy of emulation.

Mahatma Gandhi was an example. He conceived India as one integrated whole. He was highly motivated. He had a supra ordinary goal. He lived and worked with a sense of fulfillment without expecting anything except the welfare of his countrymen. If management consultancy imparts this strength to leadership development we will have an increasing number of highly productive and motivated leaders. This will occur not only in industrial and business organizations but in other fields of national importance also. Their contribution will be undoubtedly positive, productive and far-reaching. Same is the case with managers and entrepreneurs. They will be charged with the power of dynamism to make their contribution more effective and substantial.

The insights into our ancient scriptures reveal genuine wisdom, which if applied will definitely help the profession to be more effective. The offshoots of such a value creating philosophy will be of a high order. Such a list will cover time management, motivation, functional specialization, human relations, conflict elimination, ethics oriented strategy, energy conservation, cost reduction, waste elimination, human excellence etc. The philosophy definitely adds to value. It ensures better knowledge management.

The conceptual skills are embedded in works of ancient wisdom. We apply them to the enterprise and that skill becomes important for the CEO. He broadens his vision and is able to ensure and discharge his social responsibilities, which are cared for spontaneously. There will be a natural built in mechanism for resolving conflicts in organizations because the degree of understanding will be great.

Let us consider some areas where the ancient wisdom rooted in spirituality is of help to us. It clearly emphasizes the importance of goal setting for the individual. Management also stresses this whether it is an organization or a department. Individual goals crystallized will be tuned to the organization's goal and management by objectives will be better realized. The merit here is something unique in that such objectives and actions are based on ethics.

Management training is considered an important aspect of executive and organization development. This is preparing the executive for higher responsibilities. Ancient wisdom does this in a more effective way. It lays down discipline- Spartan discipline, through techniques like yoga to tune the body and health, and meditation to tune the mind for concentration. It stresses the role of positive thinking for purifying thoughts facilitating right decisions and judgment. It creates leadership models.

The kings and leaders of the past were role models and they set examples of good administration. Case studies for leadership development, duties and responsibilities and interpersonal relations, from the great epics like Ramayana and Mahabharata help to improve leadership training.

Management lays stress on training, which is equipping oneself for executive position. Ancient wisdom emphasizes equipping oneself with qualities for learning and grasping. It stipulated proper diets and physical exercise for men of action to withstand strain. Yoga is considered to be a very effective technique. It is effectively equipping oneself unlike the holiday approach of the modern executive. We applaud modern expressions like executive lunch but fail to understand the prevalence of better diet packages for men thousands of years ago.

The conceptual skills are embedded in works of ancient wisdom. We apply them to the enterprise and that skill becomes important for the CEO. He broadens his vision and is able to ensure and discharge his social responsibilities, which are cared for spontaneously. There will be a natural built in mechanism for resolving conflicts in organizations because the degree of understanding will be great.

Let us consider some areas where the ancient wisdom rooted in spirituality is of help to us. It clearly emphasizes the importance of goal setting for the individual. Management also stresses this whether it is an organization or a department. Individual goals crystallized will be tuned to the organization's goal and management by objectives will be better realized. The merit here is something unique in that such objectives and actions are based on ethics.

Management training is considered an important aspect of executive and organization development. This is preparing the executive for higher responsibilities. Ancient wisdom does this in a more effective way. It lays down discipline- Spartan discipline, through techniques like yoga to tune the body and health, and meditation to tune the mind for concentration. It stresses the role of positive thinking for purifying thoughts facilitating right decisions and judgment. It creates leadership models.

The management consultancy profession should focus on cooperation than competition. The former avoids waste and saves resources whereas the latter promotes waste and boosts up costs. Globally this principle of cooperation in lieu of competition has been accepted. That is why we have organizations like the WTO, EEC to ensure smooth economic transactions between countries.

It is beneficial to focus on self-management to promote human excellence, which is one of the most important objectives of management consultancy. The focus on training the body, mind and intellect for maintaining health, fitness, discipline, stress free existence and clear thinking for right decisions is ensured.

In all areas of consultancy the basic anchor should be righteousness. Wealth creation and acquisition should be based on this principle. This will remove greed and corrupt tendencies in organizations. It is beneficial to include among objectives of organizations the following important one- to create wealth subject to the condition that such process is firmly rooted in righteousness. The same approach is applicable to satisfying consumer desires. The availability of harmful goods and services should be restricted and gradually withdrawn.

Management consultancy is a noble profession. It can act as a catalyst to effect significant changes in standards of living and economic progress with sustainability. It should give emphasis on creating wealth in sectors where the poor people will largely benefit so that poverty will be eliminated over a period of time. All actions should be based on righteousness, i.e., fairness and transparency in dealings. Training programs should offer this as the thrust area. If this fundamental aspect is ignored the economic system will operate to the common detriment. The activities of the organization and society should be value driven and not greed driven.

This may appear to be a utopian philosophy of management. But we have to aim high and keep the ideal up and not pull it down in the name of practicality. If we do so then we are elevating the status of a thief to that of an effective, efficient and most successful manager. This is because he does not use any resources of his own to attain his objectives of stealing. Even the tools he uses are stolen. The access to concepts and methods for human excellence implied and advocated in the works of ancient wisdom confers several benefits on consultants. The Bhagavad-Gita gives us all essential knowledge for human excellence. It ensures sustainability in several areas like environment, resources exploitation, technology etc. At the individual level whether it is employee or CEO it can definitely bring results. These could be in terms of conservation of energy, resources, industrial peace, and balanced infrastructure and overall growth of the economy. Such growth will ensure equity, fairness and life balance.

Any individual who is trained with armor of spirituality will be an asset to society. He will not steal. Nor will he create law and order problems. He will enjoy life and make others happy. He will let others live happily. This is true whether he is a CEO or employee or a citizen. It is hoped the future generations of management consultants will seriously dive deep to the springs of ancient wisdom. It is our prayer that they draw as much as possible, modify and perfect them. It is our fervent hope that they will graft them into the consultancy profession so that organizations and societies benefit substantially.

15. Swami Vivekananda

"This world is the great gymnasium where we come to make ourselves strong."
Swami Vivekananda

If we are to name one great Indian who was the prime mover of world thinking on the rich heritage of India in the last 150 years the choice falls on Swami Vivekananda .There can be no other example of a vision so powerfully presented with so wide and deep an impact on humanity as that of the Swami who sowed the seeds of globalization over a century ago. The Swami by inspiration of the highest order and his intellectual acumen brought out ideas and principles many of which are of relevance to management. In this context his words implying globalization are worth remembering. These are reproduced below:

"I am thoroughly convinced, that no individual or nation can live by holding itself apart from the community of others, and whenever such an attempt has been made under false ideas of greatness, policy or holiness- the result has always been disastrous to the secluding one"

In this endeavor he firmly believed that India could enrich the world considerably. He said:
"Give and take is the law; and if India wants to raise herself once more, she brings out her treasures and throws them broadcast among the nations of the earth, and in return be ready to receive what others have to give her".

The Swami skillfully marketed the quintessence of the Vedic thoughts all over the globe. This was his vision and mission. Though he never used the term management or globalization, he was the management icon par excellence of the 19th century .He visualized the need for an inter-dependent world far ahead of the times and a global role for India.
Vivekananda was a production management wizard. He was both an entrepreneur and manager of the highest caliber. To him Knowledge was a product the nature and content of which he understood with remarkable thoroughness and precision. His product was a body of sacred thoughts assimilated from the works and

experience of the Great Masters and scriptures of this country. His mission was dissemination of vital Vedic knowledge which alone could ensure sustained harmony and progress of humanity.

India was dear to his heart. He was an excellent PRO who projected the image of India globally in the most elegant manner. He discharged the role of the Global Ambassador of India decades before diplomatic relations and foreign missions were thought of even by advanced nations.

The Swami disseminated knowledge with effective communication skills in a territory with large market potential. He realized that for sustained activity organization was necessary He learnt this from America which he openly acknowledged He demonstrated his conceptual skill visualizing the entire world as one integrated entity fused together by the concept of universal brotherhood.

He identified the market for the product in the Western hemisphere. Through excellent knowledge management skills he marketed the product globally. His photographic memory, quick assimilation, confidence, integrity, humility, fearlessness, courage, positive thinking and oratory were great assets which every leader should have.

His address at the World Parliament of Religions in Chicago in September 1893 embracing the 7000 strong elitist assembly of eminent men and women as 'Sisters and Brothers of America' created an unprecedented and lasting impact. The thunderous nonstop applause for over two minutes and the phenomenon of everyone in the audience rising to his or her feet giving a grand ovation was an acknowledgement of his powerful communication and oratorical skills. He completely relied on the tool and strength of spirituality and affirmed that India would be a world leader in disseminating knowledge in the future. His prophecy has come true now and we are all witness to this event of India emerging as a world power.

. In a short span of 39 years, reflected in his maxim "better a moment of glow than a lifetime of smoke" he unleashed a tidal wave of energy in the form of vibrant thoughts surging forth with a force that could smash stars and grind galaxies. The Swami revealed entrepreneurial traits by his decision and venture to propagate his Master's Teachings most convincingly single handed in a strange land thousands of miles away from home undertaking strenuous voyages overcoming severe obstacles often with no financial resources. He showed remarkable courage and capacity in crisis management while facing situations like the one when he lost all travel documents and letters of introduction to important personalities and organizers of the World Parliament meet when he landed in America.

He epitomized the essential ingredients of good quality leadership; These are vision and mission, value system, communication persuasive skills , knowledge of minute details, knowing something about everything including science subjects, living by example and above all surviving temptations and demonstrating courage to overcome all obstacles,.

Vivekananda left an impact on this globe with ideas and ideals which if translated into action by world leaders could transform a nation steeped in poverty to glory and prosperity. His emphasis on serving others and concern for the poor is beautifully stated in his own words.

"This life is short. The vanities of the world are transient He alone lives who lives for others. The others are more dead than alive".

This statement has relevance to social responsibilities of businessmen.

He believed in the power of youth and exhorted them to be strong to build a new India and provided the foundation for building manpower. In his words

"We want young men and women with muscles of iron and nerves of steel

He urged workers to realize the dignity of labor and have a missionary zeal.

Management profession will benefit and CEOs in particular do well to learn from his vision and mission. Some valuable lessons and underlying principles derived from his talks and works are summarized below: Individual human excellence is at the root of all progress. Spiritual strength is the most valuable strength for leaders who must have global vision. Power of thought is immense; facts are to be respected and marshaled. Self management is a precondition for success and meditation, positive thinking and yoga are tools. Strengthening the individual will make the organization strong. Core competence has to be developed with spiritual strength. Character is vital for progress. Business has social responsibility. Human mind has great potential and it can generate a reservoir of energy which has to be conserved and used for good causes. India will command respect for its treasure of knowledge.

Vivekananda firmly believed in the systems approach to human development by integrating the subsystems of the body, mind and intellect. His stress on individual excellence with the tools of self management gives proof of his concept of human resources management of the highest order.

The Swami moved like an angel in human form sweetly combining qualities of moral excellence, a piercing intellect and a large heart with concern for the entire humanity and for the uplift of the poor. Organizations failing to learn and which flouted the quintessence of the Swami's principles have landed in great crisis. Downfall of giant corporations in recent times can be attributed to neglect of these fundamental principles which were very dear to the Swami's heart. The stock market crash and the world recession are due to the greed of CEOs who apparently have become Chief Embezzlement Officers. In this context the craze of organizations to create conditions for stress and anger and then evolve stress management and anger management training programs which now assume the garb of super-specialties in the profession of management becomes redundant.

Long Live the Swami's thoughts and the power of his inspiration. May his inspiration   enhance and enrich our contribution to society by helping us to manage our resources better and productively?

16. Replace Competition

Globalization has become a universal phenomenon and even countries not favoring this earlier are now engulfed by the creed. The liberal approach to economic problems and dissemination of technical know-how and proliferation of technology are expected to boost economic development everywhere and improve the living standards of the people. Material wealth has shown tremendous increase in some countries like India and China, which welcomed globalization. There is great mobility of personnel between countries all over. In the wake of globalization the tool of competition, which has been the monopoly of capitalist economies, has spread its tentacles far and wide and shown its teeth in other countries also. It is hoped competition will ensure the lowest cost and better utilization of resources providing a wide variety of goods and services to people.

While economies have shown progress materially, by way of living standards and life styles, disparities in income have widened. It is true that many millionaires and billionaires are generated. Their life style and consumption habits increase the demand for goods and services. But for producing such goods and services shifting of resources from areas of mass production of necessities intended for the poor, to meet the requirements of the rich and the upper middle class, takes place.

This is seen in the area of housing where costs are soaring sky high making it impossible for the poor even to dream of a shelter above their heads. Costs are rising and for certain sections of the population essential goods become unaffordable. The fierce competition among business firms and their craze for capturing larger market share create the twin problems of resources crunch and high cost economy. This raises the question whether competition is a desirable philosophy in the long run for sustainable economic development.

Is there no need for new concepts and approaches to ensure equitable and sustainable development so that the benefits of growth can be shared by a larger number of people? Can economics dominated by private enterprise and competition be trusted as a reliable tool for global development considering the fact that over two billion people live in abject poverty? While competition is the essence of free enterprise should we allow this to remain in the economic scene forever as a tool of development?

Review of results and impact of competition shows merits and demerits. Competition ensures efficient use of resources because firms are forced to bring marginal resources into the production process to meet consumer needs. This is believed to ensure efficiency of the factors of production. Consumer satisfaction is another benefit assigned to competition, which seeks to satisfy needs by producing a wide variety of goods and services.

Advantages claimed by the advocates of competition are temporary and in the long run are neutralized by adverse effects. Competition brings in its train unethical practices by attempts of firms to snatch away business and market share. Bribing is one tool liberally used by many claiming to have immense competitive strength. Heavy advertising boosts up costs of marketing and the burden is ultimately reflected on the price charged to the consumer. The intrinsic value of the material is much less compared to the cost of advertisement. So avoidable wastes occur. This cost exceeds the level required to create awareness of the product among the consumers and to provide information. This danger of unhealthy competition has been recognized by international agencies. This fear has given birth to organizations like WTO.

Hence they have evolved better methods of ensuring production and distribution on global scale. A good beginning is made in this direction through cooperation. Several international agencies like the European Union; European Economic Cooperation etc give proof of this trend. This principle of cooperation has been welcomed and adopted by bodies like the WTO. In the ultimate analysis we have to eliminate competition. The main reason is that, it gives rise to strategies, which are based on expediency, and unethical practices, which are harmful to the people. It benefits temporarily firms promoting competition. Because of this many firms particularly small business firms, are thrown out of business. They are unable to command the resources on a scale required to withstand the onslaught of major competitors. So some firms close down and massive retrenchment takes place. This gives rise to unemployment.

The world is now shrinking into a global village. This situation calls for cooperative effort and cooperation has to replace competition in as many fields as possible. More organizations should be formed on the lines of WTO protecting the interests of all countries instead of allowing each to fly at the throat of others economically. Firms in the industry should organize on regional basis on the lines the oil companies have done regarding sharing and distributing their products. Such regional cooperation will definitely help to sustain all firms in the industry and make available the transfer of know-how, managerial practices and technology.

A global federal approach as in the case of multinational companies industry wise and national federal approach based on cooperation will be helpful .The units forming part of the federal organization will retain the freedom of management subject to cooperation being observed as the cardinal principle. They will consult and act on common interests and strategies.

Such a system of international and national cooperation will ensure better results and better use of resources. There will be self-regulation and saving in advertisements costs and other marketing costs. The role of governments should be to facilitate this arrangement for working such a system so that globalization with cooperation and not competition becomes the accepted economic policy of all governments. Such a world will usher in lasting prosperity for all.

17. Ethics & Human Resources

Why do problems arise in organizations or in personal life of people? There are various reasons .These are dishonesty, secrecy; personal motives etc. Over a period 'Ethics'- science of conduct, has gained importance in organizations and in human life. Ethics act as indirect governing force behind human conduct.

Ethics have gained importance with the increasing complexity of market conditions and decreasing transparency in operations, Ethics help in better decision making, lead to credibility with public and employees. Human resources are the most important part any organization. The HR department decides who should join the organization. They have the responsibility to promote ethical culture in organizations. The way the H R Department hires, fires, trains and promotes people, directly affects the employees.

Before considering ethics relating to the HR department, we shall discuss the ethics commonly applicable to all departments. First is 'courage'. This is the ability to analyze the failures. 'One must carefully learn from mistakes.' Then we take up 'commitment'. This emphasizes the clarity of organizational goals. Last is 'consensus'. This encourages participation of people and demands providing a free and open environment.

The ethical issues involved in human resources are discrimination on basis of age, gender, privacy issues, occupational health and safety, policies relating to training, development, promotion etc. Selection is the foremost task to hire people expected to render their services. This needs careful scrutiny of the application without bias and measuring aptitude of the candidate, through tests. Test must be reliable and valid. While conducting interviews, experts must not be rude, coarse, and hostile towards the candidate. Promotion is one of the very crucial areas for management and it directly affects the performance of employees. Some organizations give promotion based on seniority as a result which the ambitious and skilled workers may not show interest in refining their skills. Management must strike a balance between seniority and merit while giving promotion. Nepotism must be avoided while promoting employees as it creates distrust among employees and hampers healthy organization culture. Employee privacy is the basic right of employee. Nowadays with technological advancement, employees who use phone and computers are monitored while doing personal or business related activities. Personnel policies should abandon the use of extraordinary methods like use of secret cameras, spies and hidden microphone. Wages should be based on equity fairness and justice.

Ethical considerations should form the basis of organizations right from the top management to lower levels of management and Ethics must be well defined and comprehensive.

18. Knowledge with Spiritual Content

In the Twenty-first century we have achieved amazing progress materially in raising the standard of living of the people in general. There has been tremendous knowledge explosion and the knowledge industry is growing rapidly. The world has shrunk in terms of distances and become a village with vast connectivity thanks to the Internet and jet travel. Science and technology are advancing at tremendous speed. There is increase in GDP of most countries. Medical science has advanced and longevity of man has increased. More countries are joining the list of developed countries. Opportunities for material advancement are increasing. But can we say with certainty we have used our knowledge to improve the quality of life of man?

Have we attained the quality of life warranted by the rate and quantum of progress we have achieved? The ingredients of this are good health, positive thinking, improvement in character; compassion for others; inherent tendency and urge to help others, capacity to do one's allotted duty in the most efficient manner, maintaining a sustainable environment etc.

We are unable to make full use of the knowledge that is generated. This also raises the question whether what we acquire is relevant knowledge to improve our quality of life or harmful knowledge that adversely affects the quality of life.

Crimes of various types are on the increase. Values, which maintained the relationships in society, are declining and disappearing. We have so many specialized courses and programs of education. But they seek to improve the material advancement of man. They provide career opportunities. But they draw blank when coming to character formation, which is a major indication of man's real progress and quality of life. Have we made any progress in improving the character of man? This task is left to religious and spiritual organizations. Is not character formation an ingredient of economic development?

Progress can be sustained only if any program implemented is rooted in human character. This means a well disciplined code of conduct self imposed by the individual for the best contribution from him and for the good of society.

The ingredients of quality of life are: pollution free environment, harmonious relations within communities, decline in crime, value based leadership, a feeling of safety, absence of fear, positive roles for government, institutions, citizens, maintenance of law and order, sifting relevant knowledge and rejecting irrelevant knowledge, absence of discrimination among people positive role of media, press, films, books and substituting the philosophy of glorification of crime and immorality by that of glorification of character, contribution and social harmony.

There is dethronement of wisdom. The great and cherished treasured values are thrown to the winds by a vast majority of the population who live a life at the level of the senses. We say civilization has advanced.

Are we making any serious effort to reverse the trend except crying from roof tops that the scourge of terrorism and vice afflicts the world? Is it not time to wake up and act? We realize that cancer caused by tobacco use or smoking is an evil and treatment of this disease costs more than the revenue earned from tobacco products. Why not we realize that lack of character in humans is the chronic disease.

To reverse the trend and reduce the intensity of the damage caused why not give priority to character formation and development in all our learning and research methodologies? Why not incorporate this as an essential ingredient of progress in all branches of knowledge. There is no dearth of resources for reversing the adverse trend. Words of ancient wisdom are contained in the scriptures of all religions. We have to dig out and use them liberally. The curative properties of these works are great and marvelous and have been proved by the test of time.

Texts like the Bhagavad-Gita contain enormous potential for the benefit of mankind. It focuses only on the positive aspects and the good of man. It is a tool of motivation and human excellence. It has relevance to nation building and character and leadership development. Only men of character and vision in any field of activity, be it science, economics or politics, alone can deliver the goods on a lasting basis and ensure global prosperity and harmony. They will be anchored in spirituality. Only then we will have real progress with global harmony and happiness.

The human mind has to set its direction towards achieving this goal. It does not matter if it takes time. But the progress achieved will be lasting and solid. Otherwise we will produce more and more Nobel laureates but also a cluster of sick societies where man is preoccupied only with selfish interests, leaving the poor to their fate from which relief is almost impossible for them for decades.

This calls for the best of management of the human faculties at the individual level. It is self-management. It means rectifying the imbalance in the body, mind and intellect function. It will richly draw on the reservoir of talent and energy from inside, the God given internal resources, effectively for the benefit of society. Wisdom cannot be told. It has to be acquired through reflections on experience. This has to be done through mind control, positive thinking, and a healthy body.

We must stretch our minds to the farthest limit; take care of the body through yogic exercises, proper breathing and control of food. Yoga postures with proper breathing will ensure stamina, efficiency and good health. By living in the present we can manage time better. We can attain excellence by adding to our work age-old time-tested values. Spiritual strength that comes from the faith in a supreme power above man is the greatest asset. Man benefits by developing and holding on to it. We gain considerably if every field of human activity brings value systems in its fold.

19. Spiritual Strength & Management

In the pursuit of economic progress and higher standards of living nations often lose sight of the quality of life of citizens. There are various quality of life indices like the state of education, health, housing infrastructure etc. However, wide inequalities in income and privileges exist resulting in strife and squalor. Though the human being is recognized as an important resource, human excellence is rarely achieved except in fits and starts.

The lack of a concerted institutional approach by organizations to attain human excellence, focusing on the individual, brings about a cumulative impact pulling down the quality of life, though other quality of life indices show a positive trend. Pockets of poverty alongside oases of wealth still exist. It is here spirituality comes to our rescue imparting strength to economics and management with lasting beneficial results.

Absence of spiritual content manifests through lack of positive value systems in economic planning, business and management. The adverse effect of this omission is reflected in massive corruption, criminality, frauds, embezzlement, unhealthy personnel policies, cheating, leakages and wastages in the economy. There are also unethical practices like profiteering based on greed and dilution of quality of products and services. Often even the most competent professional who has potential to contribute to enhance the quality of life succumbs to temptations. This damages the reputation of the product and the organization he serves. Why does this happen?

Management which welcomes knowledge from all disciplines rarely seeks and applies knowledge from spiritual sources. Many consider such knowledge as inconclusive and non verifiable in terms of results. This is a fallacy. There has been no determined effort to give a fair trial to the spiritual content of the knowledge and its application to economics and management.

We manage all resources through man. The organs of action together with the faculties of mind and intellect constitute the human resource. Very little is done to manage effectively the tangible and intangible resources within man.

When we buy a home appliance or gadget we are supplied with a booklet of instructions to guide us to use it for getting the best results. Without following the contents of the booklet we are very likely to operate the gadget wrongly or damage it. While this approach is appreciated in the case of material goods and devices like VCD, TV etc., we forget or are indifferent to use a handbook already in existence for using the faculties of the human being.

Man is the most complex of all creations on this planet. Individual efforts at his improvement in some cases do take place. But many including organizations and institutions do not try seriously about it probably for the simple reason they believe such a manual does not exist.

In reality a well considered time tested set of guidelines for human excellence and happiness does exist. We don't call it a manual. It has been in existence for thousands of years in India which has a great heritage and wisdom. The scriptures contain this quintessence of guidelines for excellence. They contain principles of human conduct based on the realization of great sages who had nothing but the welfare of humanity at heart.

Of such scriptures the most important is the Bhagavad-Gita which holds the key to lift man from the worst type of depression to great heights of achievement in a convincing manner.

The Bhagavad Gita helps to effect a total transformation in his outlook and attitudes and capacity to overcome challenges of life. It explains in sufficient detail how to overcome depression, avoid stress, do one's duty with dedication, and attain human excellence. It stipulates beyond doubt what should be done and what should not be done to attain excellence. It also clearly indicates the influence of food on the quality of decision making and the thinking process to be developed. It gives the tool of meditation to avoid stress. It makes man a treasure worthy of making great contribution to the welfare of society and to himself.

Bhagavad Gita discusses various aspects of the art of man making. Management will benefit and grow if consistent efforts are made to imbibe the principles of human conduct and excellence laid down in this great scripture. If this is ignored, even if we producing probably a million Nobel laureates, economics and management will undoubtedly fail to ensure human happiness and prosperity with sustainability in all walks of life.

It is a welcome sign, a silver lining, that a few business schools have started realizing the relevance of this ancient scripture for human excellence. The world will witness faster and substantial progress if all business schools and institutions teach and imbibe the art of man making.

The focus has to be on the individual. Then the family, society, nation and the world will definitely progress. The benefits will be high quality of life, human happiness and prosperity with sustainability. The truth of this assertion is as certain as death. May the grace of the Lord be showered on all citizens and institutions of the world to imbibe this great, wonderful art of man making.

.

20. New Dimensions in Management

The science of management has made remarkable progress especially from the mid 1960s.A plethora of concepts, techniques and tools have been evolved. Material prosperity has increased considerably in countries and organizations which imbibed and implemented faithfully the new tools and techniques. But management of organizations and economies are plagued by an avalanche of corrupt and unethical practices like corporate frauds and corruption resulting in looting and wastage of national resources. Consumers are misled and cheated. Low priority goods are produced. Productivity in many organizations continues to be low and poor work culture thrives. Workers are more aware of rights and not duties. Of course there are exceptions.

Top management, employees, government and competitors contribute to this mess Right thinking managers fully armed with all modern concepts, tools and techniques feel there is a vacuum in their armory which retards real progress and achievement. This creates a deep sense of dissatisfaction and a feeling of incompleteness in their task.

On introspection they find that while efforts are made to develop resources outside man, very little is done to develop the inner resources .The ancient wisdom contained in our scriptures focuses on developing the inner strengths of the body, mind and intellect. The analogy of the human body to the chariot gives an invaluable insight. The chariot with the horses, the reins, the charioteer and the flag has great significance and a wealth of meaning for management.

The wheels of the chariot represent Dharma (righteousness) which is the foundation for other goals, namely, Artha and Kama. The horses represent the senses, the reins the mind, the charioteer the intellect and the flag with the image of Hanuman symbolizing a force overcoming obstacles with the determination to achieve the goals. The senses are controlled by the mind and the mind in turn is controlled by the intellect. Thus management functions of planning, direction and controlling are beautifully exercised.

The planning and directing function manifest in basing all actions on Dharma (righteousness). Artha or earning of wealth and Kama or fulfilling desires are subject to Dharma. This principle, if understood and faithfully followed will eliminate greed or curtail it significantly. Wealth created will be used for the benefit of a larger section of people within and outside the organization. Corporate social responsibility will be automatically ensured. It will be wealth creation with sustainability and according to priority.

The discriminating intellect sifts relevant knowledge, assigns priority, and arrives at right conclusions and sound decisions. The control function is exercised by pulling back the senses (horses) to the right track with the reins (mind) i.e. correcting deviations from the main objective.

Thus the body, mind and intellect function as an integrated system promoting human excellence and efficient management. If the concept of the chariot and its comparison with the human body is rightfully understood and assimilated by all the employees in the organization compliance of decisions will be easy and effective. With more and more employees at all levels in the organization practicing such principles the results will be better and far reaching. This perspective gives a new dimension to management.

21. 21st Century Vision

This chapter seeks to identify the basic hurdle of the consultancy profession to ensure effectiveness and results in the age of *E Governance for resource utilization and poverty alleviation.* It refers to C governance directly and indirectly promoting corporate frauds and the need for reducing political content in decision-making globally. It lays stress on imparting ethics and value systems in management *enlarging the scope of the consultancy profession* in framing solutions for the twin problems of corruption and poverty alleviation richly drawing from the treasure of ancient wisdom.

These days we talk about E Governance, which has many laudable objectives and beneficial results. Procedures have been simplified considerably. The common man has experienced most of the benefits as in the case of railway reservations. But what actually happens in many cases of administration and management is C Governance. This simply stated is

Corruption in Governance. They block the smooth flow of benefits and convenience to the common man. Corrupt practices influence decision-making particularly involving huge financial outlays. Everywhere expectations grow tall and fast but are not fulfilled. The enormous intangible resource within man, the mind and intellect, is rarely tapped and full potential realized for solving problems.

We come across cases of political corruption through the misuse by government officials of powers and the governmental machinery for illegal personal enrichment. All forms of government are susceptible to play the game of political corruption. Forms of corruption vary. But they include bribery, extortion, nepotism, patronage, graft, and embezzlement. This creates great social injustice particularly to the poor sections of the population. In some countries corruption is widespread that it occurs when ordinary business enterprises or citizens interact with government officials. The terminus of political corruption is a kleptocracy, literally 'rule by thieves'.

Corruption poses a serious development challenge. It undermines good governance by subverting formal processes. Its presence in elections and in legislative bodies reduces accountability and distorts representation in policy making. Corruption in the judiciary compromises the rule of law and that in public administration results in the unfair provision of services. It corrodes and erodes the institutional capacity of government as procedures are disregarded and resources siphoned off.

It undermines economic development by causing all round distortions and inefficiency spreading its tentacles all over the country. In the private sector, corruption jacks up the cost of business through the price of illegal payments, the management fee of negotiating with officials. Though some people observe that corruption reduces costs by eliminating red tape, the availability of bribes induces officials to devise ingeniously new rules and delays.

While corruption inflates the cost of business, it also distorts the playing field, shielding firms with connections from competition and thereby sustaining inefficient firms. Cases are not rare where firms supplying first quality products and services are disqualified in favor of those who are substandard because they could pay off huge amounts as bribes.

It also brings economic distortions in the public sector by diverting public investment into capital projects where bribes and kickbacks are plentiful. Officials dexterously manipulate and increase the technical complexity of public sector projects to conceal or facilitate such dealings.

Corruption also lowers compliance with construction, environmental, or other regulations, reduces the quality of government services and infrastructure, and increases budgetary pressures on government. Siphoning of resources and the resultant wastage thwart the main objectives of good governance. Such compliance brings forth the collapse of building structures soon after they are inaugurated with great fan fare and publicity. National poverty remains without significant change.

Economists profess that one important factor behind the differing economic development in Africa and Asia is that in the former, corruption has primarily taken the garb of rent extraction with the generated financial capital invested overseas rather than at home. Corrupt administrations in Asia have often taken a cut on everything requiring bribes, though provided more of the conditions for development, through infrastructure investment, law and order, etc.

Management consultancy, according to one definition, is: 'the creation of value for organizations, through the application of knowledge, techniques and assets, to improve performance. This is achieved through the rendering of objective advice and/or the implementation of business solutions.' Management consultants are invited into organizations to provide an objective analysis, wider expertise and independent specialist skills. They are primarily concerned with initiating and implementing organizational, behavioral and technological changes.

World economic progress, in general, during the last decade has been remarkable. Productivity and employment have increased in many fields and industrial growth has been over 9% in some countries. Globalization has brought easy and abundant availability of goods and services in the country. Some countries have moved far away from a state when gold movements took place for settling international obligations to a state where they have foreign exchange reserves of over $300 billion. The stock markets are booming with activity and massive inflow of investment from abroad takes place. But C governance also gets a boost eating away part of the resources earmarked for development.

The consultant's role and effectiveness is affected by the predominance of C-governance in all areas of activity. Sometimes client organization wants the consultant to give reports defending the decision already taken or to give a report as per the parameters set by the client, against facts, professional integrity and ethics. This prevents level playing field for those who believe in fair business practices. Thus the best of expertise on the assignment becomes non-usable. C- Governance has elevated bribing to the status of a result oriented management technique. This is particularly true in marketing. Cases are not rare where consultants are sought to do stealthily industrial espionage even by large companies. There are also cases where decisions are hurriedly taken by organizations and consultants are asked to support them by tutored and structured studies, which are based on manipulated facts.

Wastage of resource arises on account of C-governance i.e. governmental activity driven by corruption and greed. This creates a chain reaction bringing the evil effects of corruption all through the hierarchy down to the lowest level. Apart from causing depletion of resources, this promotes wide disparity in incomes and growth. C- Governance and greed of the officialdom choke decision-making and create obstacles in the way of economic progress though it is said to act as an expediting process.

The democratic system as it functions today in some countries does not permit penetration of professionalism in politics with the most appropriate skills. It is devoid of ethics. Countries like Singapore where the politicians occupying ministerial posts are high caliber professionals are few. The exclusion of politicians from the network of developing core competence for ruling the country and managing the economy distorts the system. Exceptions are rare.

This takes us to the question of widening the scope of consultancy services and area of responsibilities. Consultants are concerned with conservation and optimum utilization of resources. Does the consultancy profession have any responsibility for devising ways and means of improving performance in *developing core competence and national progress*? Of all human resources leadership is the most important. This is the core resource.

The seeds of C- governance are sown in the minds of politicians. They are nurtured by the flush of funds originating through corrupt means of party funding which is not subject to audit and scrutiny in some countries. This encourages a chain of hierarchies, creating powerful and unbreakable links with officials and donors who disrupt the sound management of the economy. The gravitational pull of such negative leadership downwards slows down progress and performance.

While there are hundreds of types of audit which have been made statutory, there is no *statutory management audit.* There is no compulsion to be efficient. It is the neglect of one of the most important areas, which could ensure productive utilization of resources for progress, and its cumulative effect that has created a huge overburden of versatile incompetence in the core sectors. Inadequacies in professional skills at the top layers of the government and the dominance of vested interests, act as an insulated shield preventing the penetration of most effective managerial tools.

Luckily the IT industry is comparatively free from the menace of political interference. Politicians do not tamper with it because many are not familiar with the complexity of the industry. Further Companies, which have achieved tremendous growth and success, attribute their achievement due to their philosophy of being value driven and not greed driven. The management of such companies has been able to resist pressures from the government officials to dilute the standard of ethics in dealings.

Can consultants in general and management consultancy in particular effectively help to tackle the twin evil of C Governance and poverty? Is there any set of effective tools they can design and adopt? If so how can it be done and how soon. Can this be made as part of the vision for the 21st century for all countries? These questions take us to the objective of widening the scope of consultancy services. The emphasis is to demolish the pillars of C governance and promote E Governance, which has brought benefits to the common man with prospects of greater benefits and convenience.

Management welcomes knowledge from all disciplines. It believes in an inter-disciplinary approach. It upholds the systems approach for solving problems. It has widely applied the systems approach for solving problems in industry. In the area of corruption and poverty elimination too there are vital subsystems. They remain outside the system and disrupt the fulfillment of the objective of economic growth with equity and social harmony. These include the politicians, the legislature and the judiciary.

One important area of knowledge demanding close and immediate attention is application of *ethics in governmental administration.* Such ethics derive strength from spirituality. In fact contrary to popular belief this is totally secular and universally beneficial. This has recently gained acceptance in western countries as a tool of managerial effectiveness. Countries and organizations where officials take orders from a situation and not from individuals have benefited from using such tools.

Concepts like Dharmic Management have surfaced and found greater acceptance. Real values of life do contain potential for improving the quality of human resource, which commands other resources. India's rich heritage and wisdom provide ample evidence of this potential. There is no need to feel shy about using such beneficial tools and management consultants can freely make use of them.

Twenty first century is going to be the century fusing economic progress with spiritual strength. It augurs well for the world economy. Countries with spiritual strength hold the beacon of hope and leadership for world development. Wisdom and the heritage of the past dating back to thousands of years teach us the art of man making. This is the unique strength India has, which others are yet to acquire. If man is developed to attain excellence, the family, society, nation, country and the whole world will attain better growth and harmony.

So the most important aspect of human development is to develop man to attain his maximum potential. His assets are the body, mind and intellect the three pillars on which his excellence is built. Intellect can be trained to develop positive thinking ensuring right decisions. The mind can be developed to imbibe values, which will benefit humanity. The body can be kept healthy so that work can be done at peak efficiency with little down time.

While developing all these aspects the unseen resource of spiritual strength - that is belief in the spirit behind the three faculties, which makes them function, is to be respected and relied upon. We may call it life, energy or consciousness. Any work in any field of activity if done with this vision will bring better results. It will make any professional a better professional in his field. It will be done with a sense of dedication. Great men and leaders who made tremendous contribution to the country were those who had strengths deeply rooted in spirituality. They were motivated to excel in their performance through a sense of fulfillment and they acted far beyond enriching themselves. Conceptual skill was imbedded in them and they could visualize the country as one integrated whole. They practiced sustainability by respecting environmental forces.

We also know the most essential things in life; air, water, space and fire are free. Without them life will be extinct. But we often forget how they came to be provided and what is the force, which sustains them. It is the realization of this truth that takes us to see and respect the spirit behind all these free resources, which are essentials and for which no monetary value can be assigned or will be adequate.

Optimum utilization of resources implies prevention of wastage. Breakdown of *law and order* is a major source of such loss. How can consultants produce maximum results in terms of national benefits? What is the most valuable tool for the consultant? Are we sincerely and steadily striving for human excellence in all areas of activity? The existing tools, techniques and concepts are inadequate. This is seen from the prevalence of C Governance and corporate frauds, which globally exist.

Some universities in Western countries are giving importance to introducing values and spiritual orientation to management practices. Consultants will benefit if they realize the relevance and strength of the core values that substantially help to attain human excellence. Is it enough if they remain in a sense of complacency entertaining the belief that the limitations cannot be overcome and they have to accept and live with them?

Ancient times witnessed rulers and leaders who were men of integrity, vision and concern for the people's prosperity with harmony. They set examples of honest living and strong concern for the people. Unfortunately there is no mechanism by which the professional integrity and honesty of political leaders is improved .Law can control only actions but not motives. Very little is done for promoting the role of character in economic development and in nation building. Character springs forth from a value system.

Just like the role of top management in ensuring good results for business organizations, political leaders have to ensure good results in ensuring good governance. This is possible only if they are well equipped. Attempts to equip them by fit and starts merely through seminars and conferences will not yield lasting results.

Consultants will benefit by undertaking research for improving the productivity of political leaders who have to be development oriented. They have to promote development leadership. For funding programs of leadership development financing by government or by large business houses can be explored.

The scope of activity of the consultants should include in-depth study of political organizations, their funding, managerial practices, weaknesses and steps to strengthen them with clear objectives in tune with the country's constitution. They are in a better position to study in depth, examine facts objectively and present findings fearlessly.

The only remedy for arresting C governance is to impart a *value system* along with other tools and techniques of management. It is not wise to equate serendipity with genius. Political leaders, who have a clean record of miserable failure in their chosen career fields, at times have shown unbelievably good results in totally different areas. This has been a subject of study and appreciation by management institutes and B schools abroad. This is laudable. But the results have to be consistent and sustained.

The factors governing success in such cases should be identified, analyzed, and used as guidance for transplanting elsewhere. If consultants can identify the causes for poor performance with a view to improve and bring out the results in public they can have an impact on the quality of governance marking a beginning of the process of demolition of the fortress of C Governance .

A well designed management control system can bring substantial improvement to minimize the impact of C governance. This facilitates early detection of fraudulent practices. This is all the more easy when real time computerized control systems are possible. Human excellence should be the goal of all organizations. Only if the top political layers in government and administration have the will to implement measures to achieve excellence, beneficial results will percolate and prevail in all organizations and hierarchies.

The management consultant has to accept a major role in national planning and reconstruction. Planning is concerned with utilizing resources most productively. The consultant's job is to ensure this by evolving tools and techniques, which include motivating men. India's *ancient heritage* upholds the cause of humanity. The concepts and principles of administration and human conduct framed thousands of years ago had that end in view. They hold good even now.

The value system definitely provides answers to many problems of administration and human relationships. They seek to ensure good conduct, fairness and equity in administration and healthy human relationships. Here quantitative and other techniques fail. We have to develop an open mind to be convinced about their worth, relevance and applicability.

We don't have to search for new tools. Actually we have only to discover the essential and most productive tools from India's ancient heritage without being prejudiced. Indian value system is the greatest global asset. It is the springboard for character formation and ultimately human destiny. This is clear from the following verse.

Sow a thought and reap an idea,

Sow an idea and reap an act,

Sow an act and reap a character

Sow a character and reap a destiny.

Management consultancy needs a wider definition to include within its ambit of operations studying the value system imbedded in our heritage and scriptures. We have to dig out and apply those with modification, convert them into productive tools to suit present day conditions. These are in the areas of time management, motivation, communications, organizational behavior, avoidance of conflict, human welfare, sustainable living standards, life balance, conservation of resources and environment.

A systems approach incorporating the value system for demolishing C Governance in organizations- political, social and economic will be productive of results. This will ensure right leadership, for thrust will be given using training methods to promote development leadership. The profession of management consultants has to go beyond corporate governance and corporate leadership. It should focus on developing leaders for political excellence.

It is essential for the healthy and sustained growth of the economy and for improving the standard of living of the poorer sections of the population that the tool of self-management techniques is given wide application by consultants. India's rich heritage with an ocean of sacred literature contains enough material for unearthing tools and concepts of relevance to modern conditions and times.

The exclusion of this factor as a subsystem for problem solving has been the cause of retrogression and growth of C governance. This lapse has resulted in system failure and retarded national progress, making it lopsided. Often, there is no national perspective and this lack of conceptual skill on the part of those running the government has resulted in more efforts and time being devoted for resolving conflicts and clash of interests.

Consultants have to widen their vision beyond the present restricted area of industry and business. *Poverty elimination* is an important area where they have to evolve new tools. *Education* is another area. Similarly with *social harmony* they have to play a role. They have to devise tools for improvements in law and order and for effective functioning of the judiciary within the constitutional provisions. Dogmas and conventional tools are becoming obsolete. We should not give a stone when one wants bread.

Consultants will do well to widen the horizon of thinking and evolve tools and techniques to tackle the problem of C governance and poverty alleviation. The concepts of *motivational economics* and *development leadership* are helpful for this. This approach has to go parallel with efforts at E governance.

While it is laudable to have billionaires among the middle class, it is also necessary in the interests of stability and harmony in society; those below the poverty level are lifted up economically. Those who manage the national economy must impart a high degree of professional *content* in decision making. The political content has to be minimized. It is this political content, of high dosage, which brings in its train all vices. It introduces unfair and unethical practices feeding the machine of C Governance causing it to spread its tentacles far and wide.

This calls for *new consultancy objectives*. These have to go beyond corporations and organizations and include political organizations particularly in the area of development leadership. The built in hurdles for social harmony and progress have to be identified, pointed out, studied and remedial measures recommended. Management consultants being a free and independent body can do this in the national interest.

Democracy does not mean willful atrophy of human faculty and potential. We should not allow things to drift. The consultants are very much concerned about their reputation to act as catalysts to produce desirable and beneficial results to their client organizations. Clients should get decisive results to benefit the organization, all employees and shareholders. The society needs to benefit by cost effective recommendations and results flowing from implementation. Policy makers have to make changes in polices to permit consultants to choose any area for study where social benefits will be considerable and in the national interest.

Statutory management audit of organizations will definitely help. This is not to develop the consultant but to benefit the nation by plugging leakages in the system of resource utilization. Academics and professionals can evolve new areas of research, which include a reliable systems approach to solution of national problems bringing in its fold the world of waste generation and willful resource annihilation.

The conventional tools apart, tools from ancient wisdom of this land can be taken and developed. This will strengthen the declaration of management that it welcomes knowledge from all disciplines and the discipline of ethics and spirituality will be brought within its fold. This will definitely be a value addition to the professional knowledge.

E governance could be supplemented and facilitated by management concepts and tools with high ethical and spiritual content to attain human excellence and resource utilization. Such concepts are readily available in our scriptures like Bhagavad-Gita On-line real time information will help to expedite the decision making process and reduce the opportunity for champions of C governance to exploit the delays converting them into money and benefits. Other measures desirable are:

Persuading national leaders to adopt management tools, which will increase the professional content in their decisions and ensure social harmony and progress?

Bringing out research findings of studies on benefits and havoc caused by good/poor leadership can help to evolve remedial measures

Seeking funds from business houses if not provided by government

Including management consultants forming units for specialized study and research on social harmony, law and order, development leadership

Forming a National Social Security Fund to benefit the poor

Substituting C governance by E governance

Imparting professional training for political leaders and Link spirituality and management to form the base for *character formation and human excellence.*

Politicians have to be professionals. They should be equipped with the concepts, knowledge, and tools including values to discharge their responsibilities to the people. Value and ethics do have a vital role in attaining human excellence, motivating the followers and conserving resources. Democracy does not advocate wanton wastage of resources by inaction and core incompetence. It does not envisage a form of government by human drainpipes. It is time to draft mature competent selective politicians as part of the consultancy profession to interact and to make them realize what professionals can do for the country.

Management consultancy should look beyond business and industry. Ethics and character come from spiritual outlook and they play a vital role in harmonious, sure and sustained economic development. This constitutes the core resource development strategy. It is developing the individual in whatever capacity he is, using the value based concepts, techniques and tools drawn from our ancient wisdom realizing the potential of the mind, body and intellect. It will help to achieve better life balance and   harmony.

21st century is destined to be the century of spirituality, which can impart great strength and purpose to human endeavor. In this area India has a great role to play and contribute to world prosperity. It has demonstrated this with the effulgence of its native intelligence and brainpower. It suits the genius of India. Its heritage depicts the finest of values systems, principles of social harmony and motivation to view performance as a source of self-fulfillment.

The heritage if rightly understood and assimilated, offers solutions to all problems of mankind. It is a question of bringing a vast number of people within its disciplined approach. The tools of mind control and positive thinking ensure productivity and equity. It helps to conserve the environment. Leadership quality will considerably improve to turn many politicians into statesmen.

Mankind owes so much to India's ancient wisdom. Works of wisdom like the Bhagavad-Gita contain teachings many of which have management implications particularly in the area of human excellence. There is nothing higher than the Bhagavad Gita as a source of motivation and excellence for nation building and leadership development. Only men of character and vision deeply rooted in sound management principles and ancient wisdom can make a nation culturally and economically strong. This is the objective of self-management.

Any activity turns more productive if spiritual strength is imparted. Management and spirituality are creative pursuits and both stress on optimum resource utilization. While the former deals with external resources the latter develops internal faculties of man.

Our environmentalists discovered the need for conservation of natural wealth only recently whereas India's ancient sages discovered and propagated this concept thousands of years ago. The mind is said to be a $10 billion gift. We must stretch our minds to the farthest limit. This is an extension of the management concept of thinking big.

Conserving our energy and cultivating positive values will greatly help the cause of management. It is the purifier, which will help to liquidate all evil tendencies in the mind. There will be no source of disturbance and one can attain great freedom from stress, which is a malady of the modern executive.

Spiritual strength is the greatest asset of any individual and nation. A manager benefits considerably and attains Total Quality Management by developing and holding on to it. Thus we achieve a better quality of life.

It is worth remembering the old saying "Better a moment of glow than a lifetime of smoke".

Management consultancy will grow by leaps and bounds and gain a lot if it brings spirituality in its fold as part of a systems approach to efficient value based and result oriented management. It is worthwhile to remember the formula practiced by the Japanese management i.e., Faith + Discipline + Hard work = Success. This if faithfully followed and with ethics and spiritual strength success will be guaranteed.

When conventional concepts, tools and techniques fail or are found too inadequate, the value system rightly tapped and utilized, will bring success.

Let us hope such an approach and a success formula will go global and will be accepted in the near future. May there be peace, prosperity and happiness to all human beings on this planet.

22. Global Happiness

Individuals need to have a global perspective to make effective contribution to the welfare of mankind. Intelligence has to be used with discrimination and man has to learn to be contented. He has to develop an attitude of working for the joy of work. Of course one should earn and get remuneration for the work done. But wealth and its acquisitions have to be based on righteousness. Otherwise greed will dominate and engulf humanity.

The recession of the last decade is an example of the global dimensions of the calamity resulting from unbridled greed. We do not wish to repeat such an occurrence. In an attitude and state of calm mind we have the answer to ward off greed and anxiety and depression will gradually disappear.

Vary rarely man realizes that life on this planet is a wonderful gift of God. We live because of His grace. We have everything needed to sustain ourselves. Mother Earth showers her generosity on us. But do we show gratitude to Him or that supreme power which makes this possible. It is a big question mark.

Man's actions amount to plundering the earth for satisfying his greed. He seems to entertain the feeling that he is the creator and all that he has is due to his effort and achievement. While giving credit to man's effort, achievements and potential every moment of our existence on this planet is subject to great risk. We consider a few examples.

Events overpower us in a moment. Tsunami, earthquake, flashfloods, accidents of all types, if reflected upon, reveal our precarious existence. Is there not a power, call it nature or God, far above us, unseen but certain, which is shielding us from greater calamities and enabling most of us to complete our life span and mission. Then why is it we don't think of that power at times at least and stand in worship and veneration.

Day to day events reiterate the fact of our precarious existence. A child playing in the street suddenly is missing. On searching for hours it is seen it has fallen into an uncovered tube well 40 meters deep. Rescue is impossible. Days of effort by several men are devoted to take out the body. All efforts go in vain. The government announces compensation for loss of life. This involves great cost.

It is the fault of the individual who dug the well leaving it opens without protection. His mind was away from the lurking danger. .He did not think about the safety of others. Another child passing and playing in the same area misses the well and is thus saved. How can we explain this strange phenomenon of death for one and escape for another. Is it His grace or man's folly or child's fate?

A bus accident takes place. Two persons exchange seats at the request of one. The person who offered to exchange the seat is killed in the accident, which occurs an hour later. The other man who did not initiate the change of seats is saved. Who saved him? These are cases where we cannot find adequate explanation. One may explain it in terms of chance.

Man faces three categories of dangers .One is within man manifesting as lack of spiritual strength, sorrow, illness and restlessness. The second one is external to man i.e., wars, conflicts, and wild animals. The third one is natural calamities: floods, earthquakes, and tsunami, tornados, collision with asteroids etc. These cannot be avoided. With the last one our strength is too inadequate and the only alternative open to us is Prayer, which is reassuring our faith in God. We implore the mercy of the supreme power to save us. The greater the intensity of our prayer the more is the likelihood of some relief. If no relief comes we develop the strength to accept the outcome as divine summons.

We all know how the entire humanity prayed when the astronauts in Apollo XIII mission faced a crisis while re-entry, a threat to their lives, over which we could do nothing else. The collective prayers of the entire humanity were answered by some supreme power and that brought back the astronauts safely. Many may explain this phenomenon as chance. But something worked when all scientific effort failed. We feel happy in believing in God and prayers. Let us maintain this source of happiness our inbuilt strength for forever.

We do not bring anything with us when we are born. We come empty-handed, live for decades, acquire many things, earn name and fame and go empty handed. It is said of Alexander the Great that when he was approaching his last days, he visualized death. The Emperor told his men to take his body in an open carriage, with hands outstretched, to send the message that he did not take anything with him. Such was the wisdom of the great emperor who conquered half of the then known world.

Instead of learning lesson from history and from experience of great men we boast, bluff, bully and bulldoze others into believing we are the source and cause of everything. While it is good to have confidence and conviction it is better to be humble and entertain the feeling we are only instruments in the hands of that great Power we call God. This attitude helps to face challenges without shocks.

This wisdom when applied is the most effective purifier. The mind and intellect suffer no disturbance. Meditation enables us to turn the attention of the mind and intellect towards a lofty but practical goal which is to be happy and contented. The body has to be maintained in good health. This is achieved through physical exercise combining proper breathing. Thus body, mind and intellect form the core assets internally demanding effective management to attain the ultimate goal of happiness. Spirituality imparts strength and vitality to this process and helps achievement.

In the pursuit of economic progress and higher standards of living nations often lose sight of the quality of life of citizens. There are various quality of life indices like the state of education, health, housing infrastructure etc. However, wide inequalities in income and privileges exist resulting in strife and squalor. Though the human being is recognized as an important resource, human excellence in the real sense is rarely achieved except through measures applied in fits and starts.

The lack of a concerted institutional approach by organizations to attain human excellence, focusing on the individual, brings about a cumulative impact pushing down the quality of life. It is true that other quality of life indices show a positive trend. Pockets of poverty alongside oases of wealth still exist. It is here spirituality comes to our rescue imparting strength to economics and management with lasting beneficial results.

Absence of spiritual content manifests through lack of positive value systems in economic planning, business and management. The adverse effect of this omission is reflected in massive corruption, criminality, frauds, embezzlement, unhealthy personnel policies, cheating, leakages and wastages in the economy. There are also unethical practices like profiteering based on greed and dilution of quality of products and services. Often even the most competent professional who has potential to contribute to enhance the quality of life succumbs to temptations. This damages the reputation of the product and the organization he serves.

Management which welcomes knowledge from all disciplines rarely seeks and applies knowledge from spiritual sources. Many consider such knowledge as inconclusive and non verifiable in terms of results. This is a fallacy. There has been no determined effort to give a fair trial to the spiritual content of the knowledge and its application to economics and management.

We manage all resources through man. The organs of action together with the faculties of mind and intellect constitute the human resource. Very little is done to manage effectively the tangible and intangible resources within man.

When we buy a home appliance or gadget we are supplied with a booklet of instructions to guide us to use it for getting the best results. Without following the contents of the booklet we are very likely to operate the gadget wrongly and damage it. While this approach is appreciated in the case of material goods and devices like DVD player, TV etc., we forget to use an already existing handbook for developing and using the faculties of the human being.

Man is the most complex of all creations on this planet. Individual efforts at his improvement in some cases do take place. But many individuals, organizations and institutions do not try seriously about it probably for the simple reason they believe such a manual does not exist.

Well considered time tested set of guidelines for human excellence and happiness do exist. We don't call them as part of any manual. It has been in existence for thousands of years in India which has a great heritage and wisdom. The scriptures contain this quintessence of guidelines for excellence. They contain principles of human conduct based on the realization of great sages who had nothing but the welfare of humanity at heart.

Of such scriptures the most important is the Bhagavad-Gita which holds the key to lift man from the worst type of depression to great heights of achievement in a convincing manner. The Bhagavad Gita helps to effect a total transformation in an individual's outlook, attitudes and capacity to overcome challenges of life. It explains in sufficient detail how to overcome depression, avoid stress, do one's duty with dedication, and attain human excellence. It stipulates beyond doubt what should be done and what should not be done to excel. It also clearly indicates the influence of food on the quality of decision making and the thinking process to be developed. It gives the tool of meditation to avoid stress. It makes man a treasure worthy of making great contribution to the welfare of society and to himself.

Bhagavad Gita discusses various aspects of the art of man making. Management will benefit and grow if consistent efforts are made to imbibe the principles of human conduct and excellence laid down in this great scripture. If this is ignored, even a million Nobel laureates in economics and management will not be able to ensure human happiness and prosperity with sustainability of the environment.

It is a welcome sign, a silver lining, that a few business schools have started realizing the relevance of this ancient scripture for human excellence. The world will witness faster and substantial progress if all business schools and institutions teach and imbibe the art of man making and include it as part of the curriculum.

The focus of effort at transformation has to be on the individual. Then the family, society, nation and the world will definitely progress. The benefits will be high quality of life, human happiness and prosperity with sustainability. May the grace of the Lord be showered on all citizens and institutions of the world to imbibe this great, wonderful art of man making.

In the twenty-first century we have achieved amazing progress in raising the standard of living of the people. There has been tremendous knowledge explosion and the knowledge industry is growing rapidly. The world has shrunk in terms of distances and become a village with vast connectivity thanks to the Internet and high speed jet travel. Science and technology are advancing at great speed. There is increase in GDP of most countries. Medical science has advanced and longevity of man has increased. More countries are joining the list of developed countries. Opportunities for material advancement are increasing. But can we say with certainty we have used our knowledge to improve the quality of life of man and his happiness? We are unable to make full use of the knowledge that is generated. This also raises the question whether what we acquire is relevant knowledge to improve our quality of life or harmful knowledge that adversely affects it.

It is doubtful whether we have attained the quality of life commensurate with the rate and quantum of material progress. Crimes of various types are on the increase. Values, which maintained harmonious relationships in society, are declining and disappearing. We have so many specialized courses and programs of education. But they seek to improve the material advancement of man. They provide career opportunities. But they draw blank when coming to character formation, which is a major indication of man's real progress and quality of life. Have we made any progress in improving the character of man? This task is left to religious and spiritual organizations. Is not character formation an ingredient of economic development? There is dethronement of wisdom. The great and cherished treasured values are thrown to the winds by a vast majority of the population who live a life at the level of the senses. We are yet to understand the implications of Aristotle's statement that law can control only actions and not motives .We don't take corrective action even after we experience failure to prevent crimes of various kinds.

Progress can be sustained only if any program implemented is rooted in human character. This means a well disciplined code of conduct self imposed by the individual for bringing out the best contribution from him for the good of society. We are not making any serious effort to reverse the trend except crying from roof tops that the scourge of terrorism and vice afflict the world. Is it not time to wake up and act? We realize that cancer caused by tobacco use or smoking is an evil and treatment of this disease costs more than the revenue earned from tobacco products. Why not we realize that lack of character in humans is the chronic disease. Why not we consider development of character as an investment proposition .It can yield good and lasting returns in terms of productivity, growth and human happiness.

To reverse the trend and reduce the intensity of the damage caused why not give priority to character formation and development in all our learning and research institutions? Why not incorporate this as an essential ingredient of progress in all branches of knowledge. There is no dearth of resources for reversing the adverse trend. Words of ancient wisdom are contained in the scriptures of all religions. We have to dig out and use them liberally. The curative properties of these works are great and marvelous and have been proved by the test of time.

Texts like the Bhagavad-Gita contain enormous potential for the balanced growth of mankind. It focuses only on the positive aspects and the good of man. It is a tool of motivation promoting human excellence. It has relevance to nation building, character and leadership development. Only men of character and vision in any field of activity, be it science, economics or politics, alone can deliver the goods on a lasting basis and ensure global prosperity and harmony. They will be effective if their actions are anchored in spirituality. Only then we will have real progress with global harmony and happiness.

The human mind has to set its direction towards achieving this goal. It does not matter if it takes time. But the progress achieved will be lasting and solid. Otherwise we will produce more and more Nobel laureates but also a cluster of chronically sick societies. Man will continue be preoccupied only with selfish interests, leaving the poor to their fate and to whom relief is a remote dream.

This calls for the best of management of human faculties at the individual level. It is the art of self-management. It means rectifying the imbalance in the body, mind and intellect system. It will richly draw on the reservoir of ideas and energy from inside effectively for the benefit of society. Wisdom cannot be told. It has to be acquired through reflections on experience. This has to be done through mind control, positive thinking, and a healthy body. It is here the concept of the chariot and its comparison with the human body becomes relevant.

We must stretch our minds to the farthest limit; take care of the body through yogic exercises, proper breathing and control of food. Yoga postures with proper breathing will ensure stamina, efficiency and good health. By living in the present we can manage time better. We can attain excellence by adding to our work age-old time-tested values. Spiritual strength that comes from the faith in a supreme power above man is the greatest asset. Man benefits by developing and holding on to it. We gain considerably if every field of human activity brings value systems in its fold.

The greater the proportion and content of noble ideas in a person, organization or government, the nobler and larger will be the benefits to society. Positive thinking benefits the individual and the nation. Negative thinking destroys both. The more the number of people and countries entertain noble thoughts and ideas the world becomes a better place to live. If it is the other way the world will be kingdom of misery despite all scientific advances and civilization. Individuals nourishing noble thoughts and ideas collectively can make a better world. That should be the global perspective. Then we will be able to ensure happiness and welfare for all.

Those who entertain noble thoughts and perform acts find joy in giving and sharing with others what they have. The affluent sections of society come forward to give part of their earnings to the poor without government intervention. The hand of the giver is always higher. It can be materials of all types or knowledge, which will make them better and useful citizens. Giving knowledge is an enriching experience. It is like lighting several lamps from a single source. The mother lamp does not lose its brightness or light when the others are lighted. Similarly when all give to one another there will be love, happiness and prosperity.

An example of positive thoughts is seen in the views expressed by the famous economist and Nobel Laureate, Jan Tinbergen.

"Generally the rich of the earth should prepare themselves for a simpler life in the future. The leading philosophy of the present, which always asks for more material goods and does not attach much value at simplicity of life or modesty in claims, has to be replaced by alternative philosophies and surely much could be learned from Mahatma Gandhi's words and example. The real values of life do contain a sufficient quantity of food and shelter; but it is not necessary to have the luxuries now aimed at. Cultural values will have to be "upgraded" again. The tremendous waste of armament and outer space research should be curtailed." While rich nations are achieving higher levels of living in terms of comforts, convenience and material possessions, poor nations are unable to maintain even the existing levels. In this context the views expressed by Jan Tinbergen is of great significance. Problems will be less and effort and energy will be available for achieving great things.